Am I A
Democrat
Or A
Republican?

-an effort to save America

Charles F. Pierce

Dedication

Dedicated to Mom, Lottie Belle Oakley Pierce Merwin
for teaching us many ways to improve the world, more by actions than by
words, all while facing mountains of adversity; and,

to family and real friends who have always been there, to dedicated teachers
and workers of every kind, to all my former students who were joys in my
life, to my family of riders on buses #106 and #112, and to every fellow
Veteran who has served or is now serving in The United States Armed
Forces.

First Edition
Copyright 2012
Harmonic Creations Publishing
8 Medallion Drive, Otego, N. Y. 13825-2122 01

Acknowledgments

Thanks to Deb Pierce Wright, my oldest daughter, for pushing me to get writing on Fathers' Day in 2011. Thanks to every person who helped me in various ways as computers, my cd player and even my watch quit! Thanks to my sister, Carol Worden, for a computer loan, to Regina Tate, who tried to put computers on more friendly terms with me, and to Sam Pollak, Editor of **The Daily Star**, for his quick cooperation. A thank you goes to **The Daily Star** in Oneonta, N. Y., for allowing me to use three editorials which capture the essence of my thoughts on those issues. A thank you goes to area young adult author Shannon Delany (**13 TO LIFE** Series) who volunteered many Saturdays last year to help 15 or 16 aspiring writers meet new tasks and challenges as our thoughts appear in written form for others to use or enjoy.

Cover design by Charlie...For the beautiful layout, prepping pictures and the cover balance picture, all on short notice, I give profound thanks to Roberta Griffith, Artiste Extraordinaire. Thanks to MaryCatherine Gohde for supplying my picture, and Mary Dyer Hannon for rooting out errors.

Through my life there have always been those who have made my life easier and better - and with big smiles. I may never have given each of you a proper thank you, but want you to know you are appreciated and loved for the person you are and have been. You make life beautiful!

Chapters

About the author

Charles Frederick Pierce, Sr. was named after his two grandfathers. He resides in Otego, N. Y. along the Susquehanna River about 30 miles south of Cooperstown, N. Y., where that river originates and flows to the Chesapeake Bay.

With coursework at The State University College at Oneonta, The College of St. Rose in Albany, and The University of New York at Binghamton, New York, he attained permanent certification in many areas of teaching including All Classes of Special Education.

His teaching was periodically interrupted as he had to leave teaching for higher pay on highway construction jobs to catch up on bills and get ahead. At one point after exporting veneer logs all over the world with his business, Pierces New Horizon Veneer, he built and ran a production hardwood sawmill just outside Otego.

For over a decade, Charlie worked mainly with quality control and safety at a Corning, Inc. disposable plastic lab ware plant in Oneonta, New York. For the first time his income allowed him to purchase a home.

Charlie had served his country in The United States Air Force in the nuclear weapons and special weapons' fields. For relaxation, Charlie plays 6 and 12 string guitars and writes songs and poetry. He also has ideas for burning water as a fuel, information he wants to get out there.

At age 70, Charlie has started writing a series of children's books putting up to five books within one cover. Topics will cover a variety of issues children and adults always have facing them in life like death of pets and people, honesty, telling lies, and treatment of others.. Am I a Democrat or a Republican? -An effort to save America, offered under Harmonic Creations Publishing, is his first book written.

Chapter 1 <u>A GLANCE AT THE PARTIES</u>

In 1933, our country had an attempted right wing coup - something I had never known or been taught. I have to admit it shook me up when it popped up during hours of online research. Is it possible the U. S. is in similar grave danger right now?

What are your priorities on Earth? Those choices have a lot to do with framing your political party choice. There are stark differences between the platforms of the Democratic and Republican Parties.

Over the past 5 or 6 decades both U. S. political parties have moved to the right drastically, right meaning more conservative. Here is the sequence of political parties from left to right.

Communist|Liberal|Democrat||Republican|Conservative|Nazi/Skinheads

The zone including the right part of the Democrats and the left part of the Republicans is referred to as the middle or the middle of the road. In the past this is where most voters normally fit in.

To the far left are *Communists,* who, after being ruled by the rich who typically own 98% of the wealth, decided to pool all their earnings then divide those earnings up in common; sort of like a big commune. A doctor is paid the same as a truck driver, and it is the State which determines who gets the training for any job. The concept of a sense of fair play may have been good in theory but Communism, in my opinion, will always fail. There are no incentives and the government controls everything - not a good set up. The sense of fair play part was great!

Liberals feel government should be more involved in seeing workers get a fair shake from the profits they produce, and if a job doesn't pay enough for basic needs, the government is needed to help make up the difference through various forms of assistance. For sure I am over-simplifying. I have heard Jesus referred to as the original liberal.

Democrats try to represent all the citizens, workers and businessmen and women, the rich and the poor under the free enterprise/capitalism economic system. There is a lot of respect for workers, for job creators and for our Constitution.

For at least a century and a half farmers represented 85% of U. S. citizens. As *Republicans*, they resented anyone not working, and living financially through government handouts as they worked long, hard days in freezing weather and under the hot sun. Congress was always good to farmers with various forms of subsidies, too. There are always a few slackers who game the system, for sure. Especially now, Republicans stand for corporations and the rich. Period. Those Republicans trying to show any compassion are minimized, ignored and trashed.

Conservatives want **no** government financial support for people, but such support is o. k. for large businesses as quiet corporate welfare. The slant was heavily to huge, unregulated companies which "should be worshipped for creating jobs." Until around 1994 Conservatives were a party with few members. Now, Republicans and Conservatives appear as a merged far right wing party with off the chart radical fascist overtones. They are fueled with massive amounts of monies from a few extremely rich supporters like the Koch brothers, and the Adelsons.

Nazis and Skinheads' territory has members who strongly want a corporate controlled dictatorship of, by and for the corporations, a concept referred to as fascism. In Italy, Mussolini, as dictator, formed the Fascist Party which Hitler quickly adopted. Fascist members show hatred to minorities, gays, the handicapped, elderly and anyone who disagrees with them.

Two major changes occurred since around 1950. Largely because of mechanization, farmers' numbers dwindled to 15% and the Republican Party, which had represented 85% of registered voters, dropped to representing 31.25% of registered voters now.

Secondly, both Democrats and Republicans have moved in leaps and gallops to the right. Except for wanting corporations to have control, Democrats have moved to the slot Republicans had held, while Republicans, at least those in office, have moved as a block into the fascist region of thinking. Everything is 'of, by and for corporations.' Workers are looked down on because they want a fair shake of the profits to meet life's costs. The Supreme Court's decision in Citizens United two years ago put that "neutral" section of our government into the active corporate category. The differences between Democrats and Republicans have never been so extreme.

Here are some typical topics which are affected by the party you chose to represent you.
- a person's right to use or not use birth control
- other women's rights
- protection by government from bad drugs, foods, toys
- propensity toward going to war quickly
- healthcare
- immigration
- the entire system of regressive taxation
- Constitutional rights' infringements like wholesale spying on U. S. citizens
- equal rights
- blind justice/equal punishments
- marijuana use
- monopoly businesses like t. v./internet/phone cable/home security
- long range planning based on scientific facts

- democracy or fascist dictatorship
- fair pay for honest work
- manipulating elections and their results
- ignoring large chunks (billions) of missing government monies
- media using publicly owned airways controlled almost entirely by one party which restricts the other party's use (radio and television)
- bailing out U. S. companies
- bailing out foreign owned businesses which have branches in the U. S.
- stimulus (using taxes paid on fuels and for road use) to fix and expand our highways and bridges during recessions or depressions
- funding education
- corporate welfare even when not needed
- welfare for poor, needy and sick
- privatizing government properties at bargain prices
- corporate use of U. S. Postal Service for almost free
- regulations on banks, Wall Street and insurance companies
- unneeded pork spending
- repeated cost overruns
- Social Security, an insurance program
- Medicare, an insurance program
- Affordable Care Act ("Obamacare")
- deliberately lying in political ads
- Citizens United decision
- government pushing religion onto you forcing your children to comply in public schools
- a President exporting many thousands of U. S. jobs to India, China, England, Italy especially during his Great Recession
- the dumbing down of candidates
- conscientious objectors
- Gestapo police on campuses and at peaceful demonstrations
- uncollected oil royalties from U. S. owned properties
- Superfund to clean up corporate contaminations
- guns to criminals without a check at gun shows
- gay rights
- tax regulations changed to require taxes on hedge fund earnings
- required taxes on every U. S. based corporation
- respect and real support for Veterans

Every one of those issues is impacted by your votes or your lack of voting. It is not uncommon for a candidate to spend what amounts to a thousand dollars or more for every vote received. If you think of it, elections are being bought by the highest bidder most of the time.

If you care, and you obviously do if you shelled out the bucks for this book, you may be wondering what you can do. Hopefully, reading this book with lots of specific examples will add to your knowledge aiding you in deciding.

I use examples because words are cheap and can be used to deceive. Long strings of provable examples can show the truth.

It's election time so expect Republicans to say, "We must save Social Security and Medicare" when they really despise them. They were very dramatic about how they felt during the earlier primary debates in 2012. Also, expect gasoline prices to drop dramatically until after the November elections are over.

We exist in a time I see as critical to the direction America will go. If protections had not been built into our laws after The Great Depression, we would currently be in The Greatest Depression instead of stabilizing, getting out of the ditch and moving forward with gains.

In the last month of George W. Bush's Presidency, America LOST nearly 800,000 jobs as we glided in a downward spiral. For the past 27 months over 4,000,000 private jobs have been added. 800,000 private jobs were added in the first four months of 2012 alone. That occurred despite total resistance by **Republicans** who **have not proposed even one jobs' bill since President Obama took office in January 2009**; and they have rejected repeated jobs' bills offered by Democrats.

Around the world and in the U. S. such jobs' bills have always been agreed upon as necessary. When you keep in mind what happened on the first day Congress was in session after President Obama took office, you can understand why. Their first order of business was to stand in front of the world's greatest legislative bodies and declare their "first priority of business" was to see "President Obama was a one term President." Not the economy, not our national security, but to prohibit Obama from succeeding at anything - at any cost. The party of "No!" has surely met its pledge while you lost your home, your job, your retirement and your hopes and dreams. Too bad for you.

Washington needs our help to get rid of the party we are paying to just say, "No," and to get us onto the same economic course we had under Bill Clinton.

You may not have approved of his personal actions but when picking a surgeon or a President during hard times, the selection is monumental. Former President Clinton says the election of Willard Romney would be a disaster for America. I strongly agree.

If Franklin Delano Roosevelt had not been elected The Social Security Act of 1935 would not have been passed into law. Had the GOP been in charge there would be no Medicare. Like with The Affordable Care Act, Republicans vigorously opposed Social Security and Medicare. If you stop to think about it, these three laws force citizens to provide for themselves as opposed to falling into line for welfare and Medicaid which are paid for by you and me as taxpayers. How is that a bad idea?

Social Security and Medicare have universal appeal. Even Republicans say, "Don't touch my Social Security and Medicare," even though they had to pay premiums as they worked for decades. Social Security, although not a huge amount to me each month, has given me a much larger sense of security than I ever imagined. It is always there. I paid into it for 55 years and am entitled to get the benefits of FICA due me.

The "I" in FICA stands for Insurance. If you paid into an annuity for 55 years would you feel entitled to get the benefits as set forward in the policy? Some will try to make you believe these come from general fund dollars. DO NOT BELIEVE LIES! The world is full of liars!

Some are opposed to The Affordable Care Act because they have been told to be... even though they like the parts of it when asked part by part. Many still have their children on their policies until 26, can't get dropped or have premiums raised, and now have no lifetime limits. Those are just three of the many parts which will benefit policy holders. You need to do your own thinking! Why don't you get angry when you are lied to by the party which says it is religious and responsible?

A 16.5% portion ($2 trillion) of GNP (gross national product-almost $16 trillion) for medical care will jump to ? 20 or 25%, who knows? It has been spiraling upward especially since 2001. Chances of getting another such bill passed, after this one took over 100 years, are very narrow, and even if it could be done, the Supreme Court is clearly with Republicans. The advantage of having the one extra vote makes all the difference in the world. Imagine a President Romney changing that advantage to 6 or 7 vs. 3 or 2.

Critical to one's lifespan is the medical care, both physical and mental, one receives. Controlling diabetes is relatively easy. Ignoring it is deadly. Medical care is like that - easy if you are pro-active and aware.
Sadly, sick people without hope, give up.

Since Social Security was enacted in 1935 by FDR, and Medicare in 1965 under President Johnson, the lifespan of the average American has been increased by ten years! To me a 15% lengthening of life in 70 years is self-evident and awesome! Both plans give us more of what we want, a longer more healthy life. Affordable Care should add to that impact.

Republicans, who voted against it, introduced over 500 amendments to stall and weaken the Social Security Bill. With over 500 amendments again, they did exactly the same thing during the development of The Affordable Care Act which became law in December 2009. Candidate Obama campaigned on getting it done and was able to do it while Democrats still had advantages in Congress. One Republican voted for it. Only one! Some day, if it survives, they will be clamoring to tell voters how much they loved and supported the bill.

A party which has done everything possible to privatize, minimize and destroy Social Security and Medicare taking "it down to the size it can be drowned in a bathtub" is the party's true position regardless what they say just before elections.

Rick Perry, a Texas governor, wrote a book in 2010 in which he told how to kill Social Security. As a Presidential candidate within the past few months he vacillated on his support according to the audience he stood before.

Some talk of "being responsible" as they lie and deceive on any and every measure.

Taking $500 billion away from insurance companies (given by Republicans in a law for no reason,) then applying it to the Medicare donut hole, becomes, "They stole $500 billion from Medicare weakening a program they say they support." The GOP just didn't want to miss the chance to rip half a trillion dollars from a program they hate - and give it to their friends at insurance companies.

Your votes in elections help determine how much longer your children and grandchildren potentially can live; or how much richer the top 2% will become.

Mitt Romney worked toward becoming a billionaire by exporting U. S. jobs; and by assuring U. S. companies will pay NO U. S. TAXES. Taxpayers end up reimbursing companies like GE for any taxes they are required to pay to foreign countries.

GE profited $5.1 billion from its businesses within the U. S., and $14.2 billion from businesses outside our borders. The company paid absolutely NO U. S. taxes! And we, Americans, continue spending billions of dollars cleaning up GE's PCB contamination in the Hudson River. It is expected to take 4 more years and at least a billion dollars to complete it.

Exxon-Mobil continues to receive a large chunk of the $40 billion in subsidies to oil companies as it gives us the finger regarding paying the $125 billion ordered by a U. S. court for its massive oil spill clean up which happened over 22 years ago near Alaska. Such gifts just don't happen, they are made to happen. Voters have picked the representatives who carefully make these and other giveaways happen.

To reverse that style, we need control of all three branches of government. We don't have enough clout to stop our government from spying on you, that program started by W. Bush, Cheney, Rove and General Michael Hayden. When the fascists attempt a dictatorial take over of America again, they will already know who represents the opposition. At that point, you will be an easy mark!

Topics like abortion and religion can easily rile up voters. Congressmen who say they are for babies and life don't show it when it comes to allowing a little critical help for babies, for instance. And those who say they are for life don't show it much when they quickly send troops to die or be maimed. Then the same representatives cut Veterans' benefits, and make them go through hoops just to get an appointment for help six months later. Too many have been committing suicide as their hopes continue to diminish. That is a national disgrace.

Taking a $5.77 trillion surplus to a $13 trillion debt in eight years is not a convincing record on which a politician should be given your vote. If an investment house did that with your 401-K would you continue to have that company represent you? At some point clear thinking must be done. Facts are pretty clear if only you will look.

Many go to a place of worship or take the family. The reasons are pretty universal with honesty and good treatment of others being among normal church beliefs. To me, a candidate who attends church then ignores everything the church stands for is such a phony. He or she is like the wavy haired minister on t. v. who smiles and smiles then slaps his wife around after church. He is slick at collecting donations. Perhaps he should be given an Oscar for acting.

When explorers came to the Americas they made disposable slaves of those living here. In Salem, Mass. some of those who came to America for religious freedoms were coerced by bullies to worship as they were ordered, the same as it had been in Europe. Bullies exist everywhere in religion and as employers. Workers had to fight for improved working conditions and pay. It cost more money to keep a slave than today's minimum wage costs an employer. Slaves and horses were given good food and medical care for it paid off in the production which resulted.

I believe there are many persons who call themselves Republicans who are decent, caring people, but have very little idea what "The Party" stands for or what it is doing. They always vote because Republican leaders always call them to assure they show up. I don't want to believe most Republicans have no respect for workers as demonstrated by the Republican Party in its attacks on labor.

Do you believe in a sense of fair play, or would you pay minimum wage and cheat on the employee's time? If an honest 90 minute movie were made showing the big differences between the two parties I am willing to bet a huge number would leave the GOP. Just the fascist thread would scare a lot of you. The attempted coup in 1933 surprised me, no, it shocked me! That coup was led by U. S. Senator Prescott S. Bush. There are more details given later on.

As a new voter, I first registered as a Conservative. I really didn't understand politics and what each party stood for. Conservative Barry Goldwater was a straight shooting person with a message of being responsible. I liked him and his style. I am financially conservative so "conservative" seemed to fit.

So if you have made a mistake in picking a party, you are not the first one. I usually am too embarrassed to admit my mistake. I don't recall much discussion regarding politics when in high school. Senator Joe McCarthy, a blooming idiot by any standards, had been attacking everyone as a Communist, and in the process had destroyed the lives of many people. It turned me off to learning about politics.

As life passes by and I see what each party really stands for, it has been easy to make an educated decision. I am a proud conservative Democrat. You can be a conservative, financially, and a Democrat, too.

With almost 200 topics identified, my plan to write a series of children's books with five books within one cover was temporarily delayed while I wrote this political book. It is important to get it completed as early as possible prior to November's election. Maybe by July 4th it will be available on Amazon.com, Barnes and Noble, Borders, Ingram, Blurb.com, iBooks,Baker and Taylor and wherever else possible. With luck it will be in book stores, too.

John Steinbeck, author of "The Grapes of Wrath," has been my favorite author throughout my life. That book in particular took us through some of the hardships innocent people suffered during the Great Depression. Our country is reliving the horrors of those devastating times now. Mom wouldn't talk about the Great Depression other than saying, "It was awful! It was really awful!" That was about all my uncles said about serving in World War II. They didn't want to relive it.

My background information comes from Newsweek, U. S. News and World Report, The Nation, Time, The (Oneonta) Daily Star newspaper, AARP Magazine, CNN, MSNBC, Fox, CNBC and The New York Times...and from numerous online articles. I have talked with many Democrats and some Republicans, and have had a lifetime of observations.

Here is a list of a few things Republicans are against.

- any regulation
- control of carbon
- Social Security
- Medicare
- Unemployment
- WIC
- Workers Compensation
- school lunches
- OSHA
- HEAP
- Taxes on the rich
- Education
- Women's rights
- Assistance for the poor
- Any plan to resolve healthcare issues
- Solving immigration problems
- Science when convenient
- Keeping infrastructure safe and updated
- FEMA, except for the rich along the Chesapeake Bay area

Chapter 2   **BUILDERS OR DESTROYERS?**

Before beginning the task of actually typing the first page of this book into a digital form I sat there giving our local Daily Star a quick read. The front page above the fold had the announcement a Dick's Sporting Goods store will be added to Oneonta's Southside Mall in time for the yearend holidays. I flipped the paper to page 10, the back page of the front section. At the top left was a picture of a man in Homs, Syria, seated on his balcony which had been blown up by troops controlled by Syria's dictator. The balcony had a simple but ornate black wrought iron railing which was likely an expensive luxury item to him. It was now twisted, pulled down by the weight of a large chunk of concrete hanging midair.

My thinking led me to wonder what we can do to improve the world by building instead of continuously destroying. We, as members of the world, need to learn to get along, and to conserve the limited resources Mother Earth has provided us. Some island civilizations died out in the past as they used up all their island's resources.

Wars use massive amounts of limited resources as does erecting, then destroying buildings, stadiums and the like. How does such wastefulness square with people saying life is precious, then leaving future life with no fuels or resources? Life is either precious or it isn't; you can't have it both ways.

Let's leave something for those 100 or 2000 or 20,000 years or more from now. Will they wonder how selfish we were?

The contrast between "building" on the front page and the purposeful "destruction" on page 10 helped in my belief: people are builders, or people are destroyers. Greed, egocentric bullying and the related politics are the major drivers differentiating builders from destroyers. Many examples will help you sort out where you stand politically.

Do humans have any basic rights - or do those with money and power dictate who can have any rights or resources needed for a safe, healthy life? My birth on August 7, 1941, started my life during WWII which I vividly remember. Basically, all my uncles were "over there." Gasoline, sugar and tires were among things one needed ration coupons to get. I stood next to our radio to listen to President Franklin D. Roosevelt and Prime Minister Winston Churchill. In response to my President's request I pulled or rolled metal and any rubber objects I could find out to a pile along NY Route 10 outside Stamford in New York. It was quickly picked up for the war effort. We were asked to send bags of milkweed pods to schools. The silky white contents were used to line flack jackets for our troops. I sent many bags in with my older sisters.

We could buy 10 cent coupons which could be used to save up for buying a war bond. Everyone bought them. I bought one from pennies I had saved. At night people gathered around an outdoor fire to share any new news about anyone killed or injured. There was no television or internet. Phones were primitive and expensive. Getting together in a group allowed mutual support for everyone, for many died from every town in the war to end all wars.

As neighbors talked they often threw war bonds or war bond coupons into the fire sacrificing even more for our country. I am not 100% sure but I think I recall throwing my coupon into the fire, too. Those fires were called "bond fires."

At the end of the war I recall people hugging and jumping up and down in the streets - dancing around jubilantly. For weeks there were many airplanes in the sky. Milk tanker drivers gladly blasted their air horns when my five siblings and I signaled them.

My Uncle Junior (Fred Oakley,) from Stamford, N. Y., wrote this poem in February 1945 at age 19 about his combat in a particularly horrible place in the Pacific during WWII.

"This Place Called New Guinea"

There's a land across the ocean
Known as God's forgotten land
Made of Mangroves, swamps, and jungles
Lofty trees and ocean sand

It is this place I traveled
On a sad December day
With the sun and heat really on me
And the devil led the way

It's a place called New Guinea
Only God and we know the way
Filled with swampy jungles
And mountains far away

It's a land full of lepers
Yellow fever, dengue too
It was here they chose to send us
We, a whole and hearty crew

Yes I saw the devil beckon
And I heard the Angels sing
I heard Gabriel blow his trumpet
And say, "Death where is thy sting?"

It's a place that God created
How He spent His seventh day
He let Satin build the framework
And let the devil have his way

Why the Japs fought to take it

Why they ever wanted the land
Why the hell we were fighting
I will never understand

Agriculture couldn't flourish
Why you couldn't grow a bean
It's the damndest piece of waste land
That I have ever seen

Let the fuzzy wuzzie's have it
Let them have their primitive way
Give it to the Aussie Lads
Let us Yanks go home today

If you ever take a notion
That afar you'd care to roam
Take a tip from one who knows
And for God's sake stay at home

For your skin will turn a deep yellow
You will have shallow and skinny cheeks
You will surely get the fever
And lie in bed for weeks

So here's to old New Guinea
It's a place that God forgot
Where the food will turn your stomach
And you'll catch the jungle rot

When my days on earth are over
And the death bells sound their knell
If upstairs is like New Guinea
Then I'd rather go to hell

When I climb the golden stairway
St. Peter will know me well
He'll say, "Come into Heaven"
I've seen you've been through Hell

Then I'll say to old St. Peter
"Say, old pal, you do mean well
But if this place is like New Guinea
I'll take the first cloud back to hell"

    Uncle Junior, like millions of poor people did, served our country patriotically wherever they sent him. Our united states were solidly locked as one, and most sacrificed a great deal.

You may think I am making this up. How can a 4 year old remember this stuff? It was very real and my mind was locked in. As an aside I also remember thinking that mountains were tall trees in the middle with shorter trees along the edge.

One final thing I remember from WWII: 99% fiercely backed the U. S. war effort, yet there was a black market whereby a person with wealth could purchase anything he or she wanted. And they did. Later, I will reveal how a very prominent U. S. Senator, whose own son was a U. S. pilot in the war, was given written warnings at least twice by the U. S. Senate to stop selling war materials directly to Hitler, goods used to kill U. S. troops; and goods we were short on. You can read the actual official warnings online.

Aircraft engineers study birds to learn secrets useful in developing more perfect airplanes. Perhaps we could take lessons from animals like squirrels which plant walnut and butternut trees which will not yield nuts until years after those squirrels have been long gone. A few days ago a local man chided me at a town board meeting when I stated exporting all forms of U. S. energy was not patriotic, in my view. Marcellus shale natural gas can be now shipped out of New York City and New Jersey ports. The first pipelines were built to those ports showing there is no intention of selling our natural gas to us.

Oil is continuously being exported around the world from New Orleans and from refineries in Texas. As our southern states suffer from the recent Gulf oil spill, an irresponsible foreign oil company, British Petroleum, takes our oil (it belongs to U. S. citizens) into the refineries, then ships the refined products around the world. Republican governors from Canada to Texas asked President Obama NOT to approved the Keystone Pipeline as it has been configured. It would be a serious threat to a very much utilized great water supply. Those southern refineries want the pipeline so they can drain and export Canada's oil, and the oil from the Balkan Fields in our northern states.

Why not build a refinery and pipeline toward all the central and northeast cities which make tires (from oil,) automobiles, heavy equipment, and on and on? Free enterprise is supposed to help set prices according to my economics' courses. Where is logic? Where is patriotism? Why are we destroying the properties of many thousands of land owners through condemnation processes to help hedge fund billionaires get richer, while keeping American oil and gas from Americans? And at very high prices as if there is a shortage? The fellow at the town board meeting told me to get used to it because that is the way it is (and the way he wants it, too!) We are supposed to be drones with handles.

U. S. coal is also being exported at rapid rates. When burned in China and India it pollutes the same air we breathe, air which blends as it travels thousands of miles a day. We can figure out how to burn coal more safely, if we have any left. Bottom line is, we are exporting our energy at rates which will leave us wanting in a few years. Japan attacked the U. S. in WWII because its energy supply was being cut off.

A glut of energy is supposed to lower oil prices from the current $102 a barrel. In the early years of this century the dictator of Saudi Arabia stated on television they would be totally happy indefinitely selling us oil at $25 a barrel. His family and a U. S. family are major stockholders together in The Carlisle Group. Saudi Arabia's dictator, whose family member is the Amir (dictator) of Kuwait, is also the major stockholder in Citibank, a company we taxpayers, under Bush, bailed out in 2008.

The price of oil is not set by competition - it is more like the pricing of peanuts, hot dogs or beer in a place like Yankee Stadium. The customers will pay what we want or go without! Hedge fund investors, like the Koch (say Coke) brothers, are allowed to buy stocks with almost no money, even though they have $50 billion. Charles and David have made significant money from you and me personally as they manipulate gasoline prices. They have been two of the biggest beneficiaries of 12 years of huge tax breaks for the rich. Additionally, several hedge fund owners make billions in profits each year and have been allowed, through a special protected loophole, to pay no taxes.

Bill Gates is the richest American. Warren Buffett is second; Charles and David Koch, who founded and fund The Tea Party, Karl Rove and many others, are third and fourth. They own The Heritage Foundation and many others I will mention later.

This book will show many specific examples of events, votes and positions which affect our lives every day, far more than you think. Many are taken directly from day to day news from television, magazines and newspapers - and from the computer. Computer sources are used mainly to expand or verify details.

Reading about what people do to each other purposefully actually made me sick as I saw what they are willing to do to fellow humans. For around six weeks I didn't even work on this project. It originally was going to be more expansive for there is a large number of items which could be written about.

I have come to command a much higher respect for elected officials who give a damn, and have to put up with such repulsive actions every day face to face. They must have a good mindset.

Chapter 3   AN ARRAY OF CHOICES

Life is about choices every day, every hour. Those choices not only affect you but usually have effects on others, too. Decisions made in the Supreme Court, in Congress and in state legislatures are the ones with the most impact on you personally. Our lives in America are vastly different from the day to day lives in Iraq, China, Nigeria, Cuba or Mexico. Mexico apparently condones private armies which kill at random without interference from the government.

Killing your own daughter for being raped against her will is not only allowed, it is an expected custom in the Middle East. The father kills her with the help of her siblings - and approval of her mother. China is transitioning from Communism, a failed system in which everyone lives in common with every other worker. A doctor, a factory worker or a cook each receives an equal share of the earnings pie. In many African countries governments are weak with hoodlums filling in the power vacuum.

The best governments survive and thrive when citizens pay attention and participate. The more wimpy citizens become, saying, "I can't change anything," the more it invites an individual or party to capture and control with an iron hand. The citizens of an Arab country which allowed a dictator to crush them for maybe 40 years made valiant attempts recently to take back their government. Thousands died or were dismembered in what was referred to as "The Arab Spring," in 2011,   as they passionately fought to the death to get a democracy similar to what America has and takes for granted.

I personally was worried for our democracy in the 1980's as a segment of our country illegally took over a part of our government by shifting taxpayers dollars into The Iran-Contra Affair; then continuously lied about it with an arrogant, "There ain't no smoking gun!"

In my earlier years we often heard of northerners flying to vacation in Cuba. Florida was more of an undeveloped swamp land at the time. Cuba thrived, even importing many U. S. made automobiles back in the 1950's. Those are the same autos they continue driving today. Again, people acquiesced allowing power to be taken by a U. S. trained person, Fidel Castro. He grabbed that power and has held Cuba hostage all these decades.

If anyone studied history he would quickly learn such a takeover can take place in ANY COUNTRY. The United States is not exempt! I am guessing enough of us would have a backbone making such a takeover a lot harder than in a weak African country. In the short run many of us would be executed on the spot which would help keep everyone else in line.

But why would YOU even allow such an event to be possible? With automobiles it is easier to add air to a soft tire than to later replace the tire and rim after paying to be towed off the Thruway. It comes down to caring and doing something as simple as voting - every time. It surely helps to be knowledgeable, too.

Following is a long list of a variety of subjects to think about. There are not necessarily wrong of right answers, but these are topics Americans are deciding or tweaking individually and as a country. As you read these I'd like you to really think how you would decide if decisions on these were yours to make.

1. Sales taxes on heating fuel
2. Wars only when necessary for America with overwhelming public support needed
3. Those who use our infrastructure the most should pay the higher rates of taxes (roads, courts, mail service, airports, weather services, canals, research, etc.) A minimum wage earner almost never uses an airport, or takes a yacht through a canal.
4. Collecting a percentage of one's earnings all his life and returning it to him in payments starting at age 62 or later to assure he provides for his own retirement (FICA-Social Security) The "I" stands for "insurance."
5. Collecting a percentage of one's earnings all his life and returning it to him starting at age 65 or later to assure he provides for his own retirement medical care at a point when he may be totally broke (Medicare) This is also an insurance program.
6. Should employees' contributions to Medicare and Social Security be kept in a "Lockbox," and if borrowed with a definite repayment plan, be paid the same interest rate we pay China? Should those funds not be included in the country's budget which has to do with taxpayers' monies vs employees' monies?
7. With an estimated 11 million illegal immigrants from Mexico who have been allowed to be here for decades with a blind eye shown, how would **you** solve the long avoided problem?
8. Should U. S. taxpayers continuously give oil corporations $40 billion (40,000 million) over every ten years as it did again a month ago in 2012? Our country is more than broke...and oil corporations regularly post obscene profits! Show me the logic! The Republicans' very next vote was to unanimously say, "No!"!!! to $10 million for WIC (Women, Infants and Children,) dollars intended to help women in rough situations avoid a possible abortion. A Republican stood and said, "With all our debts we just can't afford it." Minutes before he had voted for the 40,000 million dollar giveaway to oil companies! His real priorities were showing!
9. Can you understand how the same persons who approved and spent $2.7 billion in Iraq **every week since 2003** (through 2011) would object to a one time $2.7 billion "Clunker" program which saved millions of U. S. jobs, two of our largest manufacturers, and replaced over 623,000 gas guzzlers with efficient automobiles? Within months the money was "returned" as payroll taxes coming in replaced unemployment checks going out. Romney vocalized loudly in The NY Times and elsewhere he would "**let Detroit die!!!**"
10. Flipping or flopping, he now says his words were not interpreted correctly. How does one get "Let them die!!" wrong? Michigan gave

him a very cool reception on its primary or caucus day.

11. Should a popular yogurt corporation making enormous profits be made tax exempt, and be given taxpayer corporate welfare including taxpayer subsidies for electricity and other credits? Hurray for its success, and for the job opportunities (and great Greek yogurt,) but why does it need taxes being given it especially from unemployed and retired taxpayers? It is flush with huge profits! Businesses apparently feel entitled...and the amounts are large! I'll discuss this more later.

12. Should a Fortune Five Hundred company making over 100% profit be given taxpayer subsidized cheap electricity?

13. With every person needing healthcare, and with no person turned away when sick or after an accident, how would you assure my rights not to pay for the healthcare of others who have had a lifetime of earnings?

14. Cars weigh 1 to 2 tons while loaded trucks can weight over 40 tons. In the final analysis should car owners, or businesses pay for the costs of the extra thick, extra re-enforced concrete and steel roads and bridges needed, and for the maintenance and repairs to them?

15. Airline tickets for Monday through Friday cost more as business people dominate the ticket holders. Who should pay for the bulk of all airport costs; creation, maintenance, lost property taxes, police, snow removal, other security, etc. which now are borne mostly by taxpayers? Should those who use something the most pay a fair share one way or another?

16. Twenty-two years after the fact should Exxon pay taxpayers the $125 billion for the Valdez Alaskan oil spill as ordered by a U. S. court?

17. Should Exxon pay at least one dollar toward the $25 billion Valdez spill cleanup as readjusted from $125 billion by President George W. Bush - again leaving the bill for those of us who pay taxes?

18. Should U. S. citizens, who own the oil in Alaska, have access to our own oil instead of over 90% of it being shipped to Japan, China and other non-U. S. countries? And why, under Bush, did the oil companies pay little or no required royalties to us for the oil they took?

19. Should the Keystone Pipeline be built by illegal alien Mexicans across the United States to move Balkan and Canadian oil to Texas refineries which would then be pumped onto oil tankers for shipment to China, India and elsewhere? Within the past week CNN reported five Mexicans were arrested as illegal aliens as they boarded an airplane moving from one pipeline work location to another. We keep hearing about all those pipeline and oil field jobs for Americans, jobs Americans don't get.

20. Should hedge fund traders be allowed to continue making over one billion each year without paying any taxes on it? Several profit over a billion a year; some multiple billions! Efforts to tax them are blocked! Google it!

21. Should Republican initiated and supported 12 year tax cuts mostly for the rich, keeping trillions out of our treasury, be continued or made permanent as they, including Romney, demand?

22. Should rich earners pay a top rate of: a) 91% as Elvis did willingly

saying, "This is America - and well worth it!" b)70% as President Kennedy signed, c) 28% as President Reagan signed, d) 0% as hedge fund traders are allowed, or e) 13.9% as Republican Presidential candidate Willard Romney paid on the portions of his income he claimed as U. S. earnings? Monies (a quarter billion) in the Cayman Islands, Belgium and Switzerland apparently don't count, monies he "earned" by exporting U. S. jobs and companies which made him the most wealthy Presidential candidate - ever. I personally think we need someone who cares enough about **America** to create jobs here in the United States instead of profiting in making us a weaker nation. A strong economy is absolutely needed for a country to have a world leader status. Under President G. W. Bush, 50,000 U. S. factories were exported. Some think he and Willard are great.

23. Should a NYS nurse have to renew a license repeatedly at a cost of $50, as I've heard, to help pay off debts incurred by former Republican Governor George Pataki?

24. Should GE, a Schenectady, N. Y. company which polluted the Hudson River with PCB's, reimburse the Super Fund (meaning taxpayers) billions spent there already, and pay to finish the widespread cleanup? As one of the world's largest and most profitable companies it pays ZERO in taxes to the United States, thanks to the help of Willard Romney, while using all parts of our infrastructure. In fact, if GE pays taxes to another country, we must reimburse GE from our treasury! This is not a joke! The rich take care of the rich through legislation and The Supreme Court, too!

25. How can we stop the need for U. S. taxpayers from having to take over and pay pensions for numerous corporations which somehow "lost" the pension funds?

26. Why do NY Thruway users pay to operate and maintain the Erie Canal used by yacht owners for free?

27. Why did 45 humans lose their lives when a Thruway bridge near Amsterdam, N. Y., fell into the water after engineers warned it would happen?

28. Why did the Route I-35W Bridge over the Mississippi River in Minneapolis, MN collapse as engineers warned it would? It took two years to replace the critical bridge after 13 lives were lost and about 100 injured as it collapsed on 8/04/07. As one of the poorest rated heavy use bridges in the U. S. A., the 1964 bridge was scheduled for revamping. The George W. Bush administration and Republicans said, "No!" A bus with 60 children on board luckily didn't plunge the 115 feet as it teetered on the 1907 foot bridge. The replacement cost ended up at a figure over a quarter billion dollars - again on you and me. He spent 2 billion a week for years in Iraq, but "We can't afford it in America!" A sign on the wall should say, "Priorities count!"

WE HAVE THOUSANDS OF SUCH INFRASTRUCTURE ACCIDENTS WAITING TO HAPPEN RIGHT NOW - AS THE PARTY OF "NO" REFUSES TO RELEASE SOME OF THE MULTIPLE BILLIONS

OF COLLECTED GASOLINE AND FUEL TAXES ALONG WITH TRUCK ROAD TAXES INTENDED TO BUILD AND MAINTAIN SUCH BRIDGES AND ROADS.

CONTACT YOUR CONGRESSMEN, CONGRESSWOMEN AND SENATORS NOW SO YOU AND YOUR FAMILY WON'T BE THE ONES LEFT HANGING! And just as importantly, REPLACE those who for three years have held up such critical repairs in an attempt to sway you to make an election go a certain way; those whose only drive was to assure President Obama was not re-elected at any cost! They deserve your wrath, not your dollars and votes!

28. Why, after repeated warnings from engineers, was New Orleans flooded as predicted?

29. Why does the U. S. allow airplanes inspected in "I don't see anything" countries to operate within the U. S.?

30. Why do most airplane crashes have a known repair which was not corrected? The irresponsible companies are allowed to not only continue, they continue receiving multiple (over $40 billion since 2001) taxpayer subsidies!

31. Why are people so surprised when such accidents happen when flying "is so safe?"

32. Should Congressmen or Congresswomen get a lifetime full retirement and health insurance after serving 5 years?

33. Why are shipping containers unloaded into NYC before a possible inspection?

34. Why does Israel inspect everything loaded onto every airplane?

35. Why has Israel NEVER had a related problem? Isn't checking way cheaper in the long run?

36. Why does Israel inspect every incoming container BEFORE it leaves the country of origin?

37. With France now having 7,000,000 Muslim citizens, why did W. Bush give the contract for American airport security to a French company which paid minimum wages and hired any applicant? Would a French Muslim hire a Muslim terrorist without much thought - or even on purpose?

38. Why did President W. Bush award a top-top secret missile contract to Communist China, especially after China had stated it wanted to get into the lucrative missile business selling to countries like North Korea and Iran? And after Democrats pleaded with him not to? Congressional Republicans supported Bush 100%!

39. Why during his Great Recession did the same President send your IRS returns to India for processing with all your personal information like bank account numbers, your address, Social Security number, and a hint at your wealth, all while America was hemorrhaging jobs at almost 800,000 a month? Under Bush 50,000 U. S. factories were shipped overseas. Low paid workers in India could make much more money by selling your information so your identity could be stolen, and your bank accounts emptied! Did you vote for him? Have you

ever wondered how foreigners get your personal information? It's easy when we ship it to them wholesale so we can avoid having Americans do American work. Republicans do not respect U. S. workers who dare say we are not slaves to employers!

40.   Why did GWB give 6 of the $7 billion in the Presidential helicopter contract to England (3 engines/unit) and Italy (3 transmissions/unit?) Those completed engines and transmissions were then assembled near Binghamton, N. Y. with a one billion dollar part of the contract. This deal was not to save money; it was to hurt and punish American workers who generally vote Democratic.

With IBM and other companies gone, Binghamton is one of the most desperate areas needing jobs. Could it be because NYS didn't support Bush in the Presidential elections? Job creation is a good thing, especially here in the U. S. while we're in his Great Recession, the worst situation ever since President Hoover's Great Depression which happened after a Republican run from 1919 through 1932. Sadly people get what they vote for. That is why voters need to be informed. It took many years to recover from the Depression. The same is true after two wars, off the books' spending and repeated HUGE tax cuts aimed at the rich and corporations. A $5.77 trillion Clinton surplus became a $13 trillion debt. It was the first time in U. S. history a war was fought without RAISING taxes; and off the books,another first. Republicans made huge tax CUTS, then spent much more while choosing to collect less! In the dictionary you would read about that under the word, _____. You fill in the word.

41.   If you lost your home, your car, your job and your retirement savings, could you logically be back 100% and in good shape in three years, especially if your spouse fought you all the way?

42.   If standard procedure is to spend road and fuel tax dollars collected more intensely during recessions because everyone around the world agrees it creates factory and construction jobs very quickly, why is there strong opposition by the party of "No!" to spending those designated dollars to update our aging, crumbling infrastructure? Normally both parties agree on such spending quickly during recessions.

43.   Is more money spent on tax credits, subsidies to businesses, business tax exemptions, business toxic spill costs, buying property for businesses, building factory buildings for businesses, extending power and phone lines, natural gas lines, cable for internet, water and sewage lines, roadways, railroad sidings, sidewalks and lights for businesses, cut rate electricity and free water for businesses, police, fire and ambulance services, schooling in K-12 and college settings geared to local business needs, government retraining programs for laid off employees, government assistance in exporting, free weather service, airports built, staffed maintained and expanded with business use in mind, SBA and other free or low cost loans, patent and copyright protection, other use of the courts, military protection (especially for

oil corporations worldwide,) rescue of
business tragedies (explosions, fires, flooding, nuclear incidents,) assuming business pension plan payments, Interstate Highway System rugged enough with high enough bridges for heavy, fast moving freight, canals provided at no cost, satellites earning billions in revenues put into orbit for $200,000 while taxpayers pay hundreds of billions for the space program, medical and pharmaceutical research given without charge, farm subsidies to farmers like Congresswoman Michelle Bachmann and to Sam Donaldson, and among thousands of other things a postal system allowing businesses to send BBM (bulk business mail/"junk mail") for almost nothing, 5 cents for what you would pay at least $5.00;

OR.................

The costs of family welfare, Medicaid, food stamps, WIC and HEAP?

A clue: corporate welfare is like a truckload of sand compared with a shovel full of help for the poor and needy. Corporate welfare moves in chunks in the billions. Massive corporate welfare abounds quietly under the radar. It would take volumes of books to list them.

44. What are the reasons people usually live into their 80's now?
45. Is proactive preventative medicine more successful and cheaper than ignoring health needs until a sickness appears?
46. If you put your money into a bank saving's account should you be told, "You can't have it 'cause the bank used it for something else?"
47. If YOUR earned and TAXED money is put into the Social Security and Medicare Funds, should you be told your money isn't there and your benefits will be cut because your money was used to pay a subsidy to an oil company; or for wars which were not needed?
48. If most of the world's glaciers are now melted, low islands are now covered by ocean water, and recorded temperatures have steadily moved upward, does it make sense to think there is global warming?
49. Should a public school teacher be forced, as a condition of employment, to lead students in a religious prayer or pledge?
50. Since we are a blended country should the U. S. Pledge use "Under God" on Mondays, "Under Satin" on Tuesdays, "Under Buddha" on Wednesdays, "Under Allah" on Thursdays while omitting any added words on Fridays for those who don't believe in a religion? Rotating other names could show inclusion of Hinduism, Judaism and hundreds of others so we can equally offend every person, or in public should we leave religion out as set forth in our Constitution? Why don't people just allow every person to enjoy his or her religion without pushing private beliefs onto them? I have never witnessed anyone interrupting or interfering with someone having a private religious moment even in a public place. It only becomes an issue when someone starts pushing his or her beliefs onto another as a bully.
51. Why was President George W. Bush in favor of religion in government

here in the United States, but was insistent it would not be in the constitution in Iraq? It became Iraq's first article. It is pretty evident how religion controlling the country does not allow for a well run government, but that is what they want, and why the rest of the world makes judgments about it. Modern communication, as it is, will likely make Arabs, especially women, want a change to democracy as they see how women around the world are gaining rights.

52. Should marijuana use be on par with cigarettes and alcoholic beverages, or should users be jailed? Fact: I have never used it! Honestly. Which party (or parties) says the government should stay out of personal lives?

53. Do you know the U. S. has more jailed prisoners (at a cost of almost $100,000 each per year) than all other countries on Earth combined? I believe the world population is around 7 billion. The U. S. has less than a third of one billion. Someone is telling others how to live, for sure, maybe more than necessary!

54. Apparently other countries don't take a lot of things as seriously as leaders in the U. S. do. In Scandinavia even most killers are not jailed, but they do have to return to a restricted campus at night. I don't know all the answers but do think we need to take slow, serious looks at many such things, which if changed, could save huge amounts of money and improve our country and the world. We seriously need to stop telling others how to live.....especially while saying the government should stay out of the lives of others.

55. Schools and public buildings are designed under laws made over a century ago when heating was cheaper. The regulations assumed every possible person would breathe a gazillion cubic yards of air per hour so ceilings had to be super high, and cold "fresh" air had to continuously replace air just heated. Should a serious look be given to such designs which cost more to build and maintain - and to heat and cool? This is true with all public buildings like stores and theaters, too.

56. Would it have made more sense to have 1200 pages of controls on the $700 billion loaned to crooks at banks, insurance corporations and investment corporations instead of the three pages Bush and Paulson pushed onto Congress as an emergency? Those three pages did not stipulate the monies had to be loaned to small businesses and home owners in trouble which was the verbal reason given for the bail out. Those monies borrowed from taxpayers were loaned back to our government making an annual profit around $32 billion for the banks which had no risks in the process. The corporations paid one quarter of one percent interest while receiving over 4% on the bonds....while businesses and home owners got nothing! It is called bait and switch, more welfare for the corporations. This kind of activity is not just an occasional thing. It is happening multiple times a day. As far as the three page contract..a sixth grader would have been more competent! Bush and Paulson wrote the contract that vague on purpose.

57. Is it fair for banks to use imaginary loans from taxpayers which then get loaned out for up to nearly 30% interest? Banks can loan out multiples of monies they have on deposit within the bank. An example: with $300 on deposit the bank can loan $1000, depending on the rate set. What other business can operate like that? Imagine what would happen to you if you tried it! It represents huge corporate welfare!

58. Should over $100 billion in lost Iraq war funds, intended to buy equipment to protect our troops, be found and returned to our treasury?

59. Why does one party block efforts to do so every time such efforts are made?

60. Can you spell Swiss bank accounts?

61. Should the few thousand Oneonta City taxpayers have bowed and replaced the topsoil in Neawha Park at a cost of $250,000 as billionaire Yankees' owner Steinbrenner demanded a few years ago? It is the field where Derek Jeter played while on the Yankees' farm team before he moved to the majors.

62. Why did the Violence Against Women Act pass without a single negative vote for 12 years, then have 38 Republican men vote in unison against it last week? (April 2012)

63. Why does Rick Santorum think any U. S. citizen who uses any form of birth control should be jailed?

64. Why did a House majority leader holding a hearing on women's health refuse to allow even one woman on the panel?

65. Why did the majority not condemn a drug using announcer, a felon, when he called a 28 year old law student "a slut" when she spoke up saying another female student needed birth control medicine to control a medical condition she has? Why wasn't he fired? Why didn't even one Republican woman speak up?

66. Why did former Republican President Richard Nixon say, "Why do we waste money educating women?" Why do a large number of Arabs refuse to allow women to be educated? Do you see the similarities?

67. Should yachts, airplanes, autos, lavish "entertainment homes" and such continue to be deemed tax deduction write-offs, and be sales tax exempt, too?

68. Should shareholders be able to have a direct vote on how much a CEO is paid including benefits?

69. Should justice be equal and blind?

70. Did you know since 2010, when Tea Partiers influenced elections, over 1000 bills have been introduced in the U. S. to limit women's medical and work rights?

71. Should governors in the U. S. be able to unilaterally overturn workers' rights negotiated over decades?

72. Does free enterprise/capitalism mean all parties involved have the right to be a part of the process with input and rights?

73. Does a person's right NOT to have auto insurance trump MY right to recover when someone injures me or my property, especially when he

or she has no assets?

74. How does the right of a person not to wear a seatbelt square with the rights of ambulance workers, and towns and cities which carry all the costs of numerous accidents?

75. How can you justify texting or using a hand held phone pretty much every day while driving? Please stop before you kill yourself and/or others. Try to imagine how you would feel if such "an accident" happened to you, or was caused by you. At that point you can't reverse it.

76. Should a radio or television interviewer have more of a backbone calling out a person who is obviously lying?

77. Did you know $500 billion in Medicare funds were being given to medical providers for no reason under an obscure GOP law? And did you know those $500 billion are still in Medicare to help cover the costs of the donut hole - not stolen as Republicans repeat and repeat and repeat?

78. Do you agree we all benefit from the costs of education?

79. If one divides the gross national product (GNP) by the number of U. S. workers (about 131 million,) how much does each worker produce?

80. If an average Fortune 500 company employee yields a NET profit of $300,000 or more, what is a fair amount from that for the employee?

81. Do you agree the rich couldn't operate and make their profits without all the infrastructure and services our government provides?

82. What percent of registered voters are Republican? (31.25 and dropping fast) Sixty years ago Republicans had around 85% support. How can citizens who are being used so much take so long to see it?

83. How does such a low number of people have so much control over our country?

84. Should pathways be designated now for future Interstates, corridors which could also be used for pipelines, electric and communications' pathways, railroads and such - before buildings are built which will then need to be removed? Can you think where more Interstates are needed right now?

85. Why are post offices and businesses so top heavy with unneeded administrators who get in the way to justify their employment?

86. A class action lawsuit was brought against Hewlett Packard for purposefully programming printers to erroneously tell owners they are out of ink. They settled without admitting guilt. Did you know if you put a piece of masking tape over the part your thumb pushes when installing the cartridge, the printer can't read the information, so you can finish using those "empty" cartridges as you take the time to purchase a different brand. I will never buy any HP product again. Where are ethics today? When you buy their products they laugh at you for being a sucker.

87. After my Dell computer hard drive froze I investigated and read Dell had known it was a massive problem, according to an online story, but continued to sell millions more to our government, and millions more

to people like me. Why?

88. Did you know each state determines, on its own, what and where any pipeline will go within its state? **The federal government only gets involved if a pipeline must cross an international border**, namely Canada or Mexico. It was Republican governors who were the holdups on the Keystone Pipeline, not our President as the GOP continues to say. All states except Nebraska have signed off on the Keystone Pipeline. Speaker of the House, Republican John Boehner, has invested in five companies related to the Keystone, one being at least $50,000, according to a television newscast. He made those investments before Congressional information was released to the public.

89. Did you know the U. S. currently has more drilled oil and gas wells operating than in all the rest of the world?

90. Did you know, contrary to what the right wing says,more drilling permits have been issued since 2009 than in any Presidential four year term? Those saying otherwise are either not capable of understanding, or are lying on purpose, or both.

91. Did you know the U. S. under President Obama has more drilled wells operating than under any other President?

92. Do you know President Obama gave oil companies an ultimatum: "Either start drilling on leases (they've held for years, or forfeit them?"

93. Did you know a gallon of regular gasoline under George W. Bush ranged from $1.10 in 2001 to $4.29 in July 2008? The range under Obama is $1.95 to $3.95; $3.529 on June 28, 2012. Private enterprise with hedge fund profiteers like David and Charles Koch have more influence on the price of gasoline, even more than demand, in my opinion. The U. S. has more gasoline production now than ever even though our consumption is down, but massive amounts are being exported which is illogical to me since we are then importing to make up for what is exported.

94. Did you know when gasoline in NYS was $1.10, 50 cents was taxes, 60 cents was for the gasoline? When the price was $4.40 the tax was still 50 cents. In eight years between 2001 and January 2009, with no government resistance, the gasoline part went up 650%.

95. Can you figure why the price of a barrel of oil went from around $22 a barrel to as high as around $150......when the king of Saudi Arabia said they, the oil producers in the Middle East, would be happy a long time with a price of $25 a barrel? The Bush family was partners in businesses with King Saud. How much has that friendship/business relationship cost your family since the year 2001?

96. Can you remember the one reason the U. S. sent troops to Afghanistan, then Iraq in 2003? Why did Osama bid Laden escape from a cave in Torah Bora when he was located there? The bin Laden family is a prominent rich family in Saudi Arabia. After the attacks on The Twin Towers President George W. Bush allowed one airplane into the air, the one with the bin Laden family as they left without being asked one

question!

97. How many billions were given to Halliburton and some of its subsidiaries like Kellogg, Brown and Root, Bechtel and others for services and goods not delivered to the wars in Iraq and Afghanistan? Check out online to see how so many names associated with oil were involved, and were in the Bush administration. The U. S. was a cow to be milked!

98. How rich can a greedy distributor get by selling colored water as cancer medicine for use in America at $1995 a vial?

99. Why was BP Oil allowed to say it had plans, equipment and personnel to address "an unlikely spill in the Gulf of Mexico" without any verification under the Bush administration? Was our country being run by pre-school persons?

100. Why did President George W. Bush tell our government agencies NOT to collect royalties from wells owned by American taxpayers? Some companies aren't even American!

101. Why did the SEC, Securities and Exchange Commission, twice ignore evidence of a Ponzi scheme presented about Bernard Madoff? SEC workers were told to back off and leave investor corporations alone.

102. Why do those who conscientiously do their jobs, like the one who insisted on following the Madoff case, get fired? With the GOP in control nothing could be done to help him. Here is a simple example of what happens when you don't vote for Democrats.

103. With The Citizens United decisions legislated by The Supreme Court, do you agree North Korea, Iran, China, the Koch brothers, or any unidentified group or individual should have the right to spend unlimited money to obtain a result they want in any U. S. election? Either party can do it but only one has access to billions within an hour. Currently billionaires David and Charles Koch are funneling hundreds of millions through The Heritage Foundation, The Cato Institute, Karl Rove's multiple Crossroads GPS and American Crossroads, and many other outfits to put a positive image on Republicans. Their monies were used to take away workers' rights in Ohio and Wisconsin under Republican Governors John Kasich and Scott Walker.

104. Why don't we have a varied choice of a cable/internet/phone/home security provider as we were promised with one "super cable?" There is little or no competition.

105. What can be done when The Supreme Court Five usurps a state's right in determining its own election issue as it did in illegally interfering with an election in Florida? A high school student can tell you elections are a state's rights' issue.

106. Is smoking a personal right?

107. Does a person have the right to make the land of many people toxic when he will never have the means to correct it?

108. Do you know of any claim of being 100% safe that hasn't been proven false?

109. Have illegal immigrants been allowed to come in sort of like a ticket taker letting a child into a baseball game without a ticket?
110. Which group serves more in our military - poor people or rich people?
111. Which President stated, "You can tell what a country thinks of its military by watching how it treats them during peacetime?" General Eisenhower
112. Which President quietly cut billions from the Veterans' benefits on the day he invaded Afghanistan? GWB
113. Which party started and continuously has fought FOR Social Security, Medicare, and now, The Affordable Care Act?
114. Which political party makes an extreme effort every 30 to 45 years to bring about a recession to move wealth to the rich, and to show workers who is boss while driving down wages and benefits making people beg for a job? Historically the 1880's, the 1920's and early 30's, the 1970's and 80's, and in the first decade of this century have borne this out. Each time wealth is moved without fail. Recessions are not accidents! Republicans know "trickle down" doesn't work, but they continue repeating the theme to get the final desired result. Since unions are their biggest threat, they focus on killing workers' rights. Killing women's rights helps them, too, since many women are workers. It's also a dominance issue.
115. Why do so many people believe them just because they repeat the same thing over and over? Repeating a lie a million times does not change the truth. Liars should be pointed out and shamed!!
116. How much does a person earning minimum wage gross a year? 2000 X $7.25 = $14,500
117. How can anyone live on that, or even twice that? I have experience in very low pay as a teacher. With the time I put in I didn't even make minimum wage.
118. According to CNN how much does the average healthcare plan cost? $14,500
119. Did keeping a slave cost more than minimum wage when considering the cost of healthcare, foods, clothing and lodging even back then?
120. Is China paid a higher rate of interest on monies they've loaned us than monies taken from Social Security and Medicare Funds are paid?
121. For fun: If a century is one hundred years, what is the last year of the 18th Century?
122. Which is your number one priority if you are a Republican in Congress? a) national security b) our country's economy c) making sure a President doesn't get re-elected?
123. Do you have respect for workers who build your products, or those who serve you and clean up after you?
124. Citizens in other countries are willing to die to vote. Is voting important to you?
125. Do you really know what your party stands for - not what they say but what they actually do?
126. Do you think exporting U. S. jobs and manufacturing plants is

patriotic?

127. Is exporting our limited energy supply patriotic?

128. Does it make sense to waste energy shipping out our oil across the world, then using even more energy to ship more oil across the planet to our country from countries where some want to kill us?

129. Does physical punishment teach others to be physically cruel?

130. Should Veterans receive special privileges?

131. Should 18 year olds be able to drink alcohol?

132. Should a reliable employee expect to earn enough to be able to at least meet the costs of life's basic needs?

133. Should persons who have served their country, and built and paid for a huge part of our country's infrastructure, be jerked around and have the monies they've contributed to Social Security and Medicare disappear when they are at a point they realistically can't get a job and can't work anymore?

134. Do you know, according to a show on t. v., it costs over $5.00 per gallon for the U. S. military to protect ships carrying oil to and from the U. S.?

135. Do you think one of the U. S. political parties (not necessarily every party member) has a racial bent which exists in wink-wink type doublespeak form?

136. Why don't bullies realize people don't like to be told or forced what to believe or think?

137. Do people need to be forced to like things like chocolate or ice cream, or beautiful music, or beliefs they really embrace?

138. Should NYS taxpayers have spent multiple millions in refurbishing State owned Belmont Raceway in NYC, a place where the wealthy can hobnob? I don't know; maybe it pays for itself.

139. Is it true that for every pile of money (Social Security, Medicare, federal and state budgets, thrift banks.....) that exists there are individuals intent on taking big bites from it? Can you name at least three persons who were directors at thrift banks who never made a payment on loans they made to themselves? How many did you vote for?

140. How often were those bank director thieves successful? President Reagan and Bush, Sr. blocked criminal charges on what would have been easy convictions and collections in recapturing the "lost" monies. Are Americans accepting of such actions? These were not even legal thefts. They were felonies for which charges were never brought! Poor you if you did the same. We taxpayers had to pay at least $125 billion for the thefts. Would you vote for a governor or a President who would not repay loans in the millions, or did you? Are you beginning to see how the United States got into debt so fast? Would you hire an inept person to handle your personal money, or put money into a bank where money disappears?

141. If you could earn between a million and a billion per year would you object to paying a tax the same or higher than factory workers?

142. If the U. S. had a place like central Australia, a place which had no roads, bridges, utilities, airports, courts or government services, do you think you could start and accomplish a successful business? Also remember, no government means no established currency either.

143. Did you know the Republican (Ryan) plan proposes raising the tax on someone earning $10,000 by $112, while proposing taxes on a person earning $1,000,000 be lowered by $265,000? Should Ryan, head of the committee, be embarrassed? No, he knows it will likely go unnoticed by people who are tired from trying to work to keep up with their bills. If McCain had won in 2008, such a proposal, and lots more like it, would now be law.

144. Why was the Veterans' Administration ordered to stall and stiff troops in need of mental healthcare for many months upon returning from the Middle East between 2003 and 2008 resulting in thousands of suicides? Troops were told PTSD was a pre-existing condition, not the military's fault, thereby avoiding giving any mental care assistance.

145. Did you know you can Google "Project of the New American Century" to find out how the 2003 Iraq invasion was planned in 1997? Be sure to check the name list! You will know the names as prominent members of the George W. Bush administration.

146. Do you believe Republican Representative Allen West's statements in April 2012 that 78 to 81 Democratic members of Congress are members of the Communist Party? He had no proof whatever as he babbled on! West's actions are reminiscent of Republican Joe McCarthy's continued attacks on Democrats back in the 50's, attacks which ruined the stature of many upstanding citizens. Who would even vote for such an irresponsible *#@%? Unfortunately, some relish voting for the likes of Allen West. The same people are the ones who also believe felon druggie Limbaugh as he spews lies. When trapped Limbaugh says he is an entertainer. From what I can see West and Limbaugh both stand close to a herd of bulls; and I believe in osmosis!

147. What are your feelings about any level of government constructing a ski tow, bridges like the Tappan Zee Bridge, the NYS Thruway or an agency like the U. S. Postal Service, then selling it in a sweetheart deal for a price almost free? To me it looks like the USPS is being set up with pensions for the next seventy years prepaid, which at this point make it look like it is failing. A GOP 2006 law mandated an extra $5 billion per year in pension funds be paid NOW for pensions of workers not yet born. A really bad balance sheet could be a starting point to get us to believe it should be sold as soon as possible; and to help develop a negative public sentiment against those danged union workers who refuse to work for minimum wages.

Chapter 4   DEMOCRAT OR REPUBLICAN

Are you a Democrat or a Republican? Each party is very different, especially over the long haul. I am so embarrassed to admit I first registered as a Conservative. I am quite conservative when it comes to money things. Later, I will offer some suggestions which are simple and doable, and extremely fair to everyone.

What I didn't realize when I registered was what the Republican Party really stands for. With only thirty-two and a half percent of the registered voters, and on as downhill run; and beliefs people would run from if they really understood, Republicans need the means which will allow them to still be competitive with clout.

The expression, "The end justifies the means," sums that up pretty quickly. When they are caught in lies, they brush it off as "Everyone does it," or "You are making a mountain out of a molehill!"

Republicans know people can be riled up with religion, patriotism, and by making them think they are important when in fact they really don't care. A token Black person or a token Hispanic is thrown in right there in the front row to salvage as many votes as possible when in fact they are thinking as Republican Congressman George Allen blurbed out, "macaca!"

In the simplest words possible:
Republicans represent the rich, the corporations, or as President George W. Bush put it, "You are the Haves and the Have Mores, The Elite, my Base!"

Working persons are to be despised, looked down on. The very rich have enough resources to hire psychologists and any other persons who can figure out the best ways to proceed. One of the most perfect examples of a Republican is Willard Mitt Romney. He is so detached from "regular people," and certainly has no concept of what it is like to wonder where the next rent payment or mortgage payment is; or worry about needed health care, or food.

My three brothers and I all enlisted and served our country. Almost every person in my family, who was old enough, served in WWII. I think I have a much larger sense of what patriotism means than candidate Romney. I cannot understand how he would get up in the morning and be driven to export companies and jobs, taking them away from American workers just for money, more money than he will likely ever spend even if he lives lavishly. I would like to see him sit at a table across from each of those thousands and thousands of displaced employees one at a time. So many of them had dedicated their lives to seeing the companies they worked for be as successful as possible. In my opinion calculating behind the backs of those employees to take their jobs so he could stuff more money into his pockets, is a very big form of being a coward. Years later, employees being interviewed will, without question, NOT vote for "the lowlife who stabbed them in the back and took their livelihoods with a series of lies." Such are the stories which are used to show moral or immoral examples down through time.

Perhaps the Veterans returning from several stints in Iraq and Afghanistan would have been able to apply at those companies if they were still here. Romney really doesn't care, anymore than Ohio Governor John Kasich, or Governor Scott Walker of Wisconsin, who vehemently went on a union busting expedition a year ago. I actually feel sorry for them because they don't have the depth or capacity to really appreciate how hard workers are committed to doing a job with immense pride. Republicans represent those with money. Period!

What Romney and Bush did to America is more offensive to me as a Veteran than I am allowed to express in this book. I would tell them to their faces!

Democrats represent all the citizens, even the rich. That does not mean taking wheelbarrows of money to them day after day. Democrats have a deep sense of our rights, our security, and of human needs like medical care, food, shelter and safe products.

I do not know a single Democrat who is a Communist, or is for giving money to a free loader. None! That "liberal" label is used heavily meaning "Communist" or "Pinko" as Democrats were called when I was a child. If you get down to it, "Jesus was the original liberal!"

Workers were paid so little years ago they couldn't save for retirement. At a point as we age, we really can't keep up, and if we try it hurts continuously. Workers got old, couldn't work and couldn't pay the bills, especially medical bills. Since 151 other countries had already had "Social Security," Democrats took the initiative to say, "Workers should be forced to save for their own retirements so as not to impose onto other citizens in their later years."

Social Security was started by Democrats and has been fought continuously by Republicans. In effect, employers have to give up a little more of their immense profits because workers fought for raises to meet their basic needs.

Also, after The Great Depression workers started to organize and realize how many profits they were making for the company. Medicare is also an employee earned benefit, a program forcing workers to contribute to their own medical needs during their retirements. Both Social Security and Medicare contributions are earnings which are taxed. Employers are required to contribute, also, from the profits the employees produce. The "I" in FICA (Social Security) stands for "insurance." These are insurance programs.

You buy auto insurance and home owner's insurance, and hope you never have to collect or use those insurances. With Social Security and Medicare you have a good chance of receiving benefits. A few don't benefit, but that is the nature of insurance.

At age 70 I have now been paying much more in Medicare premiums every month than I have benefited. I likely haven't benefited over $100 in the past year. My part of the premiums is twice that per month, but if I should need medical care, it is comforting to know I can get that care.

Throughout my life I have seen so many people go without healthcare because of the costs. Very sad cases. Death is often the answer or result.

I waited to start Social Security, too, because I was still working. I never realized how secure it would make me feel. If it hadn't been invented and started I would suggest it. It isn't that much, especially because my teaching career started with a pay rate of $5200 per year. It really revved up and zoomed all the way up to $18,020. That was possible because I tutored for the school, too, and was the only bus driver substitute for all the routes at that school. Oh yeah, I also got $100 a year for being the Ski Club Advisor and chaperone for a year. Insulting Republicans rant on about teachers being paid so much. Yeah, right!

Unless a person takes the time to read and study politics he or she slides into a party without giving it much thought. From birth through high school persons are subjected to politics directly and indirectly by hearing their family's discussions. It is pretty natural for children to assume the same beliefs and attachments their parents have in religion, politics, sports' teams including NASCAR, and in forms of punishment. Those hit by a belt or given hot sauce tend to use the same tactics. When I watched my sixth grade teacher pull one's ears, or whack a student's knuckles hard against a desk I made a personal vow NEVER EVER to repeat her bully measures which at that time were accepted punishments. Bullying and forced physical control over others actually fits into politics. Those who feel they are smarter and the only ones who know what's right, feel they must show the "dumber people" how things should be done.

Those who assume the same political persuasion of their parents do it without much thought. Besides not knowing what they really believe, they ignore the slow 'drift' in beliefs which has been massive overall in the past 5 decades. In many ways Democrats have drifted hard to the right except for going gang-buster overboard for the rich and corporations. Such a drifted condition made me roar with laughter two years ago when a "REPUBLICAN" Tea Partier carried a sign with the words something like, "And keep your hands off my Soc. Sec. and Medicare!" How is that in demonstrating a confused person in terms of knowing about political parties. She wants Democratic values while supporting Republicans. You just can't pan gold from a sawdust pile!

Through former House Majority Leader Texas Republican Dick Armey the Koch brothers financed a strong start of The Tea Party. Not knowing the origin, my interest was piqued, that was until I researched it. Where was The Tea Party from January 2001 through January 2009 when real spending was going on. As I am sure you recall, Clinton left a $5.77 trillion surplus. In 8 years Republicans took that surplus to a $13 trillion debt with tax cuts for the rich and wild spending and giveaways. The originating Tea Party leaders were part of that eight year spending spree! I know I am writing this same thing more than once. I hope I will find the right context for you to really get it. The interest on that spending is a trillion a year now. Guess who are now saying President Obama is putting us into debt by a trillion dollars every year! Is that called Archie Bunker thinking?

The term "Follow the money" works mostly every time. The money IS the right wing, and the Kochs, with Grover Norquist, who wants Social Security and Medicare to be damaged enough he can "drowned it in a bathtub." Social Security and Medicare are both employee earned and paid programs started by Democrats. Over the decades Democrats have defended them while Republicans do everything possible to destroy them, all while saying, "We must save Social Security and Medicare!" George W. Bush tried to get the funds put into the stock market where the money would just disappear. Now the GOP leaders want to give out vouchers. Either way is like taking a chainsaw to the programs.

That brings me to this point: citizens join a party based on sound bites which are often misleading; or out and out purposeful lies. I dislike "lie" or "liar," but it is the most exact description, and it is well deserved when a candidate says something like,"Democrats stole $500 billion from Medicare" full well knowing the $500 billion were subsidies snuck into a bill to give those Medicare funds to medical related companies for absolutely no reason, well except maybe some good paybacks during election times.

The $500 billion never left Medicare. It was reassigned to make the donut hole smaller; nothing was stolen. If you recall during the Bush administration Congress was in session many nights until 5:00 A. M. Bills were switched, even after voting, to those which included language for those giveaways to pharmaceuticals and insurance companies. There was no democracy, just arrogant, oppressive, total control as in a dictatorship. The GOP knew senior citizens who watched C-Span carefully would be sleeping.

Is that the party you want to belong to? It might be noted Republican candidates and/or their pacs receive massive election funds from pharmaceuticals, oil companies and health insurance companies. A few million dollars per candidate is nothing when compared with the gross funds those companies handle.

As large piles of money accumulate from American workers contributing to the Medicare Fund, more and more privately owned basically useless rehabilitation centers and hospitals are opening. Our population is aging. My brother was in a rehab center which boasted it had all the modern state of the art equipment and employees. As weak as he was, my brother was so angered he asked, "Where is all the therapy I was told I'd get if I came to this facility?" From that day things improved - about 2%.

My aunt is in a rehab center with charges purported to be around $1000 a day from Medicare. The doctor ordered four main things in writing: 1) regular ice packs on the area of the broken bone, 2) assisted walking at least early A. M., in the afternoon and again in the evening, a minimum of 3 times a day, 3) professional physical therapy, and 4) a diet for a diabetic.

Her meal when I arrived was French fries, a heavily bread encrusted piece of fish, corn, and a square of cake with one quarter inch sugar frosting. Although she had been there two full weeks most days she had no walks even when she asked.

When put under pressure an administrator unbelievably defended their actions by saying walking a few feet to the sitting room to eat counted as a walk even though it was done in a wheelchair without ever standing up. Most days her requests for ice packs were ignored. Employees would leave to get the ice and never return.

Professional therapy amounted to a small velcro weight placed on each ankle after waiting one half hour, then continuing to sit there in the wheel chair with 50 other patients. Her only instructions were, "Lift your legs one at a time." It was her arm that needed therapy. For over a thousand dollars a day I would expect a chauffeur, steak and lobster, drinks and a show by Elvis. Clearly this multi-floored rehab center was a Medicare milking machine! The patients at this Syracuse "facility" were anything but the primary concern. The facility owners and employees should be ashamed!

It seems everything is a scam today, and it appears to get worse by the day. It happens because Congress and YOU allow it!

Less than one-third of registered voters control America more and more. Their numbers are dropping so their methods are becoming more intense to make up for it. Their motto is: "The end justifies the means." They do what they "need to" and are not embarrassed knowing they continue to win, even win big in tax cuts, etc. I am sure they laugh at those who let them get away with such actions. I am also sure they have pride in being able to smooze the herd.

Money helps keep people disciplined. The GOP members are able to maintain and control the election process even calling on the Supreme Court "Five" to assure a close election. They get out and vote EVERY TIME something Democrats don't do. In effect, we acquiesce to their power grabs. Eight years allowed appointments so a 5:4 ratio exists; 5 Republicans:4 Democrats.

In Congress every Republican votes in unison to keep a tight grip. "I'm too busy to vote," not voting, or voting based on false stories has taken our country to the brink of a world depression. People with good, truthful information make better decisions. A few minutes now and then to learn can easily save you your job, your house or other rights which have no price tag. Since actions really do speak louder than words, a large part of this book will show specific actions or votes taken which will help you see how each party votes.

As we approach a November in a Presidential election year, Republicans, who really hate Social Security and Medicare will be out there saying, "We must save Social Security and Medicare!" If a race is close somewhere we will see Republicans in those districts actually voting for some things working people want just to help capture votes. The Massachusetts GOP senator, who took Senator Ted Kennedy's seat, does that regularly. He has quiet approval from his party to do that because the end justifies the means. Otherwise, he votes in unison with them every time.

Humans and animals each have basic needs, with food, water and shelter being the quickest to come to mind. Nature has a way of dealing with animals if such items are missing or not adequate - the animal fights for something like food, or simply dies.

As humans we must follow laws, fighting or killing for foods is not allowed. Stealing someone's lunch or shoplifting is a short term remedy, for sooner of later the person will be caught.

Despite good planning and responsible living almost every person or family hits an unexpected rough patch and comes up short on basic necessities at some point. Good credit can get you by as long as you still have a job, the means of repaying. Savings are also a fall back but statistics show most, unbelievably, have not accumulated a very good reserve.

Without going into detail suffice it to say employees only receive 10 to 15% of net profits they generate for employers. A very large percentage cannot pay for the family's basic needs even if those employees are 100% responsible financially. If animals they would just parish.

Slave owners took care of slaves they owned the same as farmers assured their horses and cattle stayed in excellent health. Slaves may not have been served prime ribs but they were given a sufficient diet along with lodging and clothing, and good healthcare for sure. So what do humans do when they can't afford basic healthcare, housing or food needs even though they work hard and work overtime?

Programs like food stamps and HEAP are set up as subsidies for what businesses don't pay their employees. Taxpayers can be forced to pay but employers are not! The old idea of being paid according to "a sense of fair play" does not work when the employer's mind is only in a greed mode. Although it is hard for me and many others to believe a human being would treat another human in such an inhumane way, it is so. Romney clearly stated, "I'm not worried about the poor people!" indicating they can find help if they look around. He also said, "I like to fire people!" Those two comments are very telling about his detachment to reality and human needs. And these were television versions of what he really thinks.

In the 1980's air traffic controllers were being forced to work outlandish overtime in a job riddled with stress. They were not looking for higher pay, just the hiring of more controllers to reduce expensive O. T. and the associated stress. Lives were in the balance if they screwed up on the job. The stress was causing a very high divorce rate, drug and alcohol abuse, even suicides.

Macho Republican President Ronald Reagan, who had served the Actors' Guild as its president, fired almost every controller when controllers decided to stand their ground using their rights to bargain for working conditions. The only President I am aware of who slept through several infrequent Cabinet meetings was given hearty slaps on the back with words like, "Good going, Mr. President!" after his unpredicted firings of thousands which left airports short of essential employees, and flyers at risk. The consistent disdain for working people by Republicans is unbelievable and overwhelming! Asleep at the Wheel was likely distracted about additions to his acquired California land and home donated to him illegally by a wealthy supporter who had undoubtedly received favors.

An Alaskan Republican U. S. Senator was charged and convicted for similar additions to his home in Alaska. Many Republicans worked day and night to get the conviction(s) overturned. Why wasn't Reagan arrested and tried, too, for that, and for Iran-Contra? Martha Stewart, a Democrat, who also broke the law was tried, convicted and imprisoned. In school I had learned justice was supposed to be equal and blind.

I watched an unknown poor woman with children sent to jail for writing a check for around $100 for food for children when she had no money. Blind, fair, equal justice? Whose crime was greater: lying about national security, or stealing needed foods for children? According to society's laws, they were both wrong, both crimes. The mother cried intensely as the Republican judge reamed her for stealing something not hers.

Reagan stole millions. We taxpayers paid for the multiple millions of dollars of additions to his property which were supposed to be secret. As when he lied about national security/Iran-Contra, no charges came forth. Isn't it odd the same people who got so uptight when President Clinton lied about a personal issue which was nobody's business, were totally silent when Reagan **repeatedly** lied about national security; and about where our taxpayer dollars were going illegally?

Following those lies Congressional Republicans unanimously renamed The George Washington International Airport for Reagan. President Washington's heirs were dismissed by Republicans when the Washington Family said they objected because they had legally donated the land for the airport on the condition it would forever bear the name of George Washington, a U. S. hero and its first President, a man who actively fought in a war for America. Republicans gave them the finger. As one who watched Republicans for many years, the arrogance displayed was expected as normal, but was still repulsive, very repulsive.

The evolution of the Democratic and Republican parties has had many twists and turns. In text books and online there are tons of writings if you are one who likes to get into the nitty-gritty details. There are too many to include so I'll give an overview here.

From around 1830 when the Democratic Party was started, it dominated as the successful party over the Whig Party with continuous narrow victories. The Democratic Party is the oldest U. S. political party. Originally, it was the Democratic Republican Party; then the Republican part was dropped. Thomas Jefferson was our first Democratic President.

Democrats represented farmers, city laborers and Irish Catholics opposing Whigs, who represented elites and aristocrats, and the Bank of the United States as it advanced by taking advantage of small farmers. Democrats had control of New York, Pennsylvania and Virginia, the 3 most populous states back then.

Whigs and Democrats, according to a computer writing, were both divided over the slavery issue. As the Whig Party fizzled its members joined the newly formed Republican Party which was almost identical in its thinking and support.

Republicans continued the Whig push for Prohibition, the outlawing of drinking alcohol, somehow thinking they had the right to take away the rights of others.

In my mind I see that as a continued thread of bullying. Similar elements had lived in Salem, Mass. where they had a practice of putting a woman "witch" into a burlap bag with a live cat before throwing her into a pond. Women were also burned at the stake by those men who knew they were the smart ones who had to do their duty bullying, oops, controlling the dumber ones, especially women! Keep in mind women have had the right to vote for only 91 years, since August 26, 1920.

Negative feelings toward women having any rights is a fallback to what men thought of women for thousands of years. A woman in the Middle East cannot vote, cannot receive an education or drive an automobile, cannot leave home without permission, must walk behind a man if allowed to go somewhere, must cover herself with a burka, can be stoned to death by her family if she is raped, is told whom she will marry, and can be divorced if her husband says, "I divorce you" three times. In some parts of the Middle East women have increased their rights somewhat. I am no expert but with Matthew, Mark, Luke and John as starter books, I believe The Bible was totally written by men.

I would be willing to bet $20,000 (not really) that all religious books were written by men. Even The Bible indicates women should be kept in their place. I see Republicans as those who look down their noses at women, not every Republican, but a common theme exists within the Party. Republican President Richard M. Nixon was quoted as saying something like, "Why do we waste money educating women?"

If The Bible books were written up to a thousand years after Christ died, how were those writings anything more than the opinions of the men at that time in history? Would a book written in 2012 square with books written 1500 years ago? Can you now understand inconsistencies within The Bible? And wouldn't it make quite a difference who wrote it, even in 2012? I have the feeling Jesus would have a lot to say to those who use his name in politics as they hoard to the rich forgetting the needs of the poor, the sick and other unfortunate persons I would love to hear Republicans defend themselves as they explain how compassionate they are!

A life of a human being is precious yet even in this century millions have been sent into war knowing many will die; and all that done at the drop of a hat so a relatively few rich persons can become attached to oil rights. Why aren't those lives precious? Why aren't the lives of babies born into poverty precious?

Fifteen minutes after Republicans passed a $40 billion subsidy for oil companies they voted as a block to deny $10 million to WIC, Women, Infants and Children. That defines "precious" for them!

40,000 million : 10 million "We just can't afford it!" he said so seriously!.

Such votes are the real proof despite whatever words they say about loving life and being Christians. Try to imagine a book of Santorum, or

Romney. Willard has been a strong follower of the racist Mormon religion for decades. It has only been in recent years they have openly backed down on the racist element within their studies. You can Google it. As former President Clinton said, (paraphrased) "The election of Romney will be a disaster to The United States." As a Rhodes Scholar he has been spot on every time he discusses an issue. I think racism is a large element in this year's Presidential election.

Abraham Lincoln, a Whig and a U. S. Congressman from Illinois, became a Republican as the Whig Party collapsed over the slavery issue. **In 1860, Republicans dominated northern states as "Northern War" Democrats. They backed military intervention in the slavery issue. I have read Lincoln didn't really care one way or the other over slavery, but with the Presidential election outcome to be determined by populous northern states he logically knew he'd have to resolve the issue which boiled on everywhere. Thus he decided to free the slaves.** That isn't exactly the way I was taught in school. Apparently **being the Party of Lincoln means being an opportunist.**

The Civil War lasted from 1861 through 1865. Afterwards, southern whites resented Reconstruction and the Republican Party, seeing Lincoln and Republicans as the ones who messed with "their rights to own slaves." *In 1872, with a Republican depression*, Democrats won although Republicans kept the White House until 1884. The poor citizens backed Democrats; *the rich backed Republicans, as usual, richer from a depression.*

Republicans continued for decades pushing for Prohibition which they were finally able to impose on citizens in 1918 as a Constitutional Amendment passed. It was repealed 14 years later in 1932 as power was taken from Republicans for bringing about the worst economy the United States has ever had; maybe even the world. The stock market had crashed in 1929. It was a time for the Mellons, the Rockefellers and others to acquire massive fortunes.

Top rated stocks were purchased for a penny or two as former home owners warmed themselves around a burn barrel as banks boarded up their former homes. That is still going on here in the U. S. A. as I type in 2012. Someone or some of about 300,000 persons should be ashamed, but they are too busy counting their money!

Poor and working people had nothing after the crash. Money doesn't disappear; it moves from one to the other. According to a television newscast $27 TRILLION moved from the poor and middle class to the top 2% during George W. Bush's Great Recession. That included properties, stocks and retirement and pension funds. Pretty much everyone lost. I know I did.

From 1910 to 1916 Democrats were for stronger antitrust laws and regulations, opposed Prohibition, spoke for programs for farmers who were hurting, and for rights for railroad workers. Just like now in 2012, the rich, corporations and Republican leaders ranted on about regulations which would "kill jobs." Anyone with a hint of sanity would know corporations, especially banks and the stock market, needed and still need regulations. They push every limit every time. It is not a time to believe in "Trust me!" Look at the damage they have done then and now.

From 1919 through 1932 German Americans shifted to Republican; Irish Catholics, a dominant segment of Democrats were ineffective, and Republicans controlled and went on a roll representing the rich and corporations taking our economy into the Great Depression.

How could anyone be surprised now when the same actions brought about The Great Recession? It would have been much worse if stop gap measures had not been established over the years, measures focused to thwart such a total catastrophe. That old expression, "Those who fail to learn from the mistakes of their predecessors are destined to repeat them," is exactly right.

With predictable results, the stock market crashed in '29 leading to strong support and a landslide win for Franklin Delano Roosevelt in 1932. Hoover's run with solid Republican backing had done its damage!

F. D. R. campaigned on relief for unemployed, economic recovery, and building in measures (regulations) to prevent such a recurrence. Regulations were to take away the "wild west" approach to economics which, as evidenced, methodically destroyed the golden goose egg through extreme greed. A sufficient profit was not enough. Every possible ounce of profit was squeezed from diligent workers who were subjected to great known risks on the job. FDR was elected by a landslide majority begging him to please change things so a depression could never happen again. He picked up the ball, made changes and restored hope. Many people who could not face having lost everything jumped off buildings to commit suicide. The situation was tense.

Like soldiers who returned from war not wanting to be reminded of what had happened, my mother, when asked by me about the Great Depression, simply stated, "It was awful. It was really awful!" That was it. I felt the impact of those words - and still do. I remember the pensive tone vividly. I never asked again. Mom's family was a large one with most being school age at the time. For decades citizens wouldn't put their money into stocks.

Favorable IRA's, including Roth IRA's, and employee deductions into a stock plans in later years coaxed workers to again put money into corporations only to be beaten again at the beginning of this century. All the normal rules about investing in the stock market don't apply any more. Especially with the advent of computer trading. You cannot beat those who vacuum all loose change and profits from all the stocks big and small, good or bad. They have it perfected.

Roosevelt's plan was referred to as The New Deal. Those who supported Roosevelt's plan were referred to as "liberals," a term the GOP constantly throws out there as a derogatory term. It is like the term, "Communist," they used to throw at Democrats. In April 2012, Florida Republican Congressman Allen West, who was forced out of the Armed Forces for shooting his issued pistol in an unsafe manner while on a personal vendetta, proclaimed, "78 to 81 Democrats now in Congress are registered Communists!"

Labeled "Insane" in a Florida paper he offered no proof, not even for one case. Pathetic is pathetic, and he is pathetic! He expects you are stupid enough to believe him as he continues in his ranting attempts to discredit Democrats. He is another of their wacko members like Dan Burton.

The sting from The Great Depression stayed in peoples' minds for the balance of their lives. I imagine anyone who has lost his home, his job, his life's savings and retirement in recent years through Republicans' Trickle Down Economics/Tax Cuts For the Rich nonsense, will think more than twice before he or she votes again for a Republican; that is unless massive negative ads sponsored by billionaires are believed over real facts. Some voters are not competent to see through the negative ads.

Some unfortunately, will vote Republican even if they lost everything. In America that is their right. Limbaugh makes them somehow believe the Easter Bunny is real! Were people smarter back in 1929? Their resentment was real and long lasting. They got it!

At this point if you are reading this book there is a chance you will vote for Democrats because you appear to want to find out things about current politics. Your vote IS VERY IMPORTANT! *You must know that!*

Now more voters come along who fall for the billionaire Koch (say Coke) brothers Tea Party noise which has the same elements which lead to the '29 crash. For crying out loud! Open your eyes! And your mind. Do you really want to lose your job, home and retirement if you haven't already?

Despite Republican yammering, the First New Deal reached out to business and labor, farmers and consumers, cities and countryside. The "Second New Deal" in 1934 aimed more at organized labor, nationalized welfare by the Works Progress Administration, set up Social Security, and increased taxes on business profits. Results' bearing jobs like building parks we still use today, were done through public works programs to help meet the very basic needs of millions who could find no jobs. I believe the Works Progress Administration was also referred to as the CCC, or Civilian Conservation Corp. Besides planting many acres of trees, they built the local Gilbert Lake State Park in Laurens, N. Y. Having no money to spend lead to less production. The cycle fed on itself and had to be reversed through financial stimulation, an accepted practice worldwide, then and now.

Reforms were made for banks, the stock market and in other areas, even controls on prices of products. Again, Democrats were "hired to fix the economy," as former President Bill Clinton said. "Here's another Republican mess to clean up!"

With worldwide exploitation of workers by the rich and corporations, Communism's popularity jumped around the world. 98% of money was controlled by the top 2%. The unwillingness to share enough of the profits with the workers frustrated citizens worldwide.

Some countries nationalized everything sharing the profits "in common." Under Communism every worker is paid the same; a doctor is paid the same as a custodian or a logger. The government decides what a person's job is to be. Perhaps the reasoning to share was right, but to me a system without incentives will create some slackers. We see freeloaders on Dr. Phil's shows, those content to sit on a couch and play games or watch television while contributing nothing.

Theoretically capitalism should work until you consider big money can and does control whatever it wants to control. An employer which doesn't get the employees it wants, has to add some incentives like money and benefits. A person who has spent 4, 5 or 7 years and $80,000 or MORE for college takes a minimum wage offer as an insult. If employers have the right to set pay rates, employees have the right to say, "I'm not working until we come to a workable pay agreement." Too often an employee cannot even recover the costs of going to college. That is ridiculous! With the Republican Taylor Law, I would lose that day's pay plus three more days' pay, a total of 4 days' pay, if I stood my ground and didn't show up at work even if we didn't have a contract.

Well, that law is tailored to the employer which has no penalty even if the parties don't come to an agreement for 5 years or longer. Retro pay doesn't include interest either. School boards appear to be run mainly by Republicans and with one major focus - to keep professional certified teachers' pay levels down. Most pay levels are considerably under what a factory worker makes, a worker who doesn't have to have passed kindergarten.

Seldom are any provisions made for improving the lives and pay of teachers. Many are forced, as I was, to go work on highway construction or work in a factory to catch up on bills and build toward a retirement which could provide basic needs. In both instances I made over twice what I was paid as a certified special education teacher with multiple permanent certifications. A couple Republicans have told me, "You knew what you were getting into, so you have no beef!" I can say, "No, I didn't. In no way did I expect professional teachers as a group to be held down with such low compensation." We always have to fight for little steps in pay.

As an attorney, Abe Lincoln said something like, "My time (and advice) is my living!" Although teachers enjoy their work, it is not a hobby. Show some respect at negotiation time!

Last year with 18 years of credits and at age 69 I applied for my teacher pension. I was floored when told my pension would be $88 a month; but to receive that I would have to add even more of my money, around $2400 for arrears upfront. I would have to live over two years before I retrieve my new contributions! Would you agree this is an insult to a teacher, or to any worker?

While teaching, a percentage was deducted from every check, too. NYS just added a Tier VI which will assure even lower pensions. I hear rants about public workers' pay being obscene. Those who say that are obscene.

A guy who can hit a ball with a stick can receive $20 million a year, or for part of a year. It would take a $35,000 teacher 571 years to earn what a sports' figure earns in one season. People have choices, priorities. Education has no priority when it comes to paying for it, but for sports, concerts or NASCAR "Here is my money!"

How many of you have spent more money on one such sport weekend than on your entire school tax bill? Such thinking is a form of greed, the results of which you forced upon my family. How many of you protested spending $4 trillion on Iraq and Afghanistan since 2003? Again, it is priorities. The result is teachers get fed up and must leave in an attempt to meet basic needs. School taxes are the only tax a voter has a direct vote on. Voters take out all their anger on that vote.

Writing these pages doesn't bring me happiness. I can hope a better informed citizenry will vote in more of an educated manner to prevent our country from going into an even worse situation. Writing each item causes me to relive the horror or stupidity of it. It is hard to acknowledge to myself item after item the fact persons who are supposed to be chosen, qualified representatives of ours, deliberately choosing to jeopardize our very existence - on purpose.

I understand discussion and disagreement. Democrats do that within constantly. Some see that as a weakness, yet one Republican will state what all Republicans are to think and like lemmings, all fall in line without any question or input. Somehow that doesn't seem to be the purpose of paying most legislators over $200,000 when extras are added to the base pay. The GOP for more than a decade has had almost a 100% voting record in accordance with whatever the GOP leader stipulates.

It sickens me to realize I put my life on the line by enlisting to support such actions. The statistics elude me, but few Republicans, percentage-wise, have served in our military. Poor persons and minorities enlist the most. They tend to be Democrats. But it's the voters who have been the reason such obstructionists are controlling pretty much everything. W. Bush had veto power for his 8 years. From 2001 through 2007 the GOP also controlled the House and the Senate.

Briefly until Senator Kennedy died Democrats controlled the Senate with 60 votes, which then reverted to GOP control. Voters chose to add a large number of Republicans to the House in 2010, while Democrats held a simple majority, but not a 60 vote filibuster-proof majority in the Senate.

I see Democrats basing decisions on facts and truths.
Republicans make decisions based on convenience and politics influenced heavily by wealth and greed.

AN EXTRA FACT: According to Pew Research on Google only 6% of scientists are registered Republicans. Scientists deal with truths.

Chapter 5 <u>**OVERCOMING THE GREAT RECESSION**</u>

There are some things on Earth which are constants; no matter where you go these things reside - good or bad. Lying, stealing, a lust for power and a lust for wealth (greed) are some of those constants which will always be in every society. Some countries have better controls with laws and the enforcement of them. Others are more like the wild west with few or no protections. In either case those with great amounts of money have distinct advantages. Those with few resources have to be tuned into earning enough to meet the costs of basic needs, so time constraints keep them from being aware of a lot of what goes on around them locally and nationwide.

Liars are everywhere with varying reasons for their actions. One may make up elaborate, vicious stories to maintain her job and health insurance while pregnant and about to lose her job. A child may be embarrassed and deny stealing some cookies. A drug addict lies and denies constantly.

People steal because they are lazy, because no matter what they do they can't get ahead enough to pay for basic needs, because they see something they can't resist, or for a million other reasons. The lines for stealing are blurred somewhat when laws are vague, purposefully written just right to allow the theft to be legal.

Norton-Symantec billed my credit card for a multiple year subscription without my permission. When I give an authorization I always stipulate, "This is a one time only authorization." They apparently kept my card number and information on record, then decided to go ahead with criminal use of my card. I wonder how many millions were also billed similarly, and how many paid it. It took me around 10 months to clear it from my charges. Norton had no proof for there was none. I intended to not continue with that company.

To uninstall a program with my permission should have been a quick event. Why did it take them two days and a lot of grief on my part to uninstall their security program? I certainly felt harassed! I already had another security program available ready to install. If a company is vindictive and unprofessional how can it be trusted to have anything to do with your computer or with mine?

I can answer the question, "Why do we have so many regulations?" We need the regulations to prevent corporations from jerking us around, billing us illegally, selling printers programmed to say you are out of ink when you are not, and on and on.

Regulations don't stop them from going illegal. The most they get usually is a slap on the wrist, if that. The customer is lucky if the government even gives them a phone call.

In baseball the umpire makes calls one way or the other. There is no, "You ran well so I'll say you are safe this time." When that is done the other side gets hosed.

Fines to companies like Norton should be automatic and sharply increase if the issue isn't corrected immediately with no follow up complaints. If Norton had to pay me, the customer, $100 and the government agency $100 for every incident reported, all troubles would be stopped immediately. There is no use in hiring agents to protect us if they don't show their teeth and represent us.

Sleazy outfits don't get a second chance with me. I have tried to delete AOL's trial offer. After I uninstalled the only AOL related program, AOL evidence still pops up. I don't want it, I don't want to be bothered and I don't want it taking up space in my computer. There is a computer printer company whic**H P**rograms its printers in advance to tell you your printer is out of ink when it is not. I yearn for a time when corporations are honest and don't play games.

Just yesterday I learned I am not covered by the Medicare insurance company I elected to cover me since January 1, 2012, because "You haven't activated your insurance." They verified I had paid for January 2012 in November 2011, and every month since then by their companies' monthly withdrawal from my checking account the amount of $171.25. Without my realizing it, Medicare, itself, became my default carrier and had been the entity which paid a couple small claims under $200 total. The giant company has continued taking my money right up to date, so far. The total taken is $1198.75. How many other people who thought they were covered has this been done to? I have had two persons in the know ask me why I haven't stayed with Medicare in the first place. "You don't need to go with a commercial carrier. You can still elect to buy a supplementary company to pay what Medicare doesn't, and you can elect to buy drug coverage, if you wish." We need to unite against the commercial carriers which have as their only motive producing profits. The carrier I thought I had, had its profits increase around 45%, according to a CNN newscast.

There appear to be no ethics. I now need to stop the authorization, and reclaim my money. If I died while this continued, those funds would be taken without any question. There are so many confusing decisions to make when it comes to Medicare, and at a time retired people just want to relax without the stress. The greedy insurers know that and take full advantage. They represent Republicans, and donate heavily to Republican candidates.

Even though I used the printer very little I had to replace 7 ink cartridges within a year. I printed only a total of 100 pages max of typical typed single-sided documents during that year, and it was with the expensive paper which is supposed to take less ink. There were no pictures printed.

After I covered the info on the cartridge (where your thumb pushes the cartridge) with opaque tape, I was able to use the balance of the ink in each cartridge before I started using a new competitive brand. Now I use the original printer only for an occasional fax.

I bought a computer and pay a monthly internet connection charge for the purpose of researching, sending and receiving e-mails, etc. I do not want any company capturing my computer's screen space, memory and a portion of its computing capacity. I have not bought from any of those advertisers and never will. The internet provider sets up multiple ads with moving pictures which download and appear before I am allowed to access what I want to do. I have protested to them with no changes. And remember I am paying them, in my mind, to be able to do what I want to do. Where is a regulation which would require the internet provider to gain my permission before they get in my way? Imagine having to listen to a minute or two minutes of ads preventing you from using the phone service you paid for monthly before you could call 911 during an emergency. The idea is the same.

We were promised competitive services and prices over a cable for years before it was installed. According to former Corning, Inc. CEO, Amo Houghton, Japan's citizens pay $20 a month for unlimited, worldwide television, worldwide phone, and worldwide internet; and it is incredibly fast. U. S cable companies have monopolies in segments they have divided to avoid competition similar to what the oil companies have done in laying out their sales areas.

How about a simple universal approval form of 50 words of less when a simple approval is needed for using something like a computer program? Why is a 5000 word contract needed, contracts which realistically no one reads? You could be agreeing to give your car to them.

When I have a choice among companies, I tend to go with an ethical company which also helps me conserve my time by not wasting it. Why is it so hard to get them to give the price or the shipping costs without digging?

Our country has been moving ever so quickly toward being Scammers, Inc. Everywhere companies are still reacting to having eight years with no regulation enforcement. Vendors know many customers will pay $50 or more in charges which are known as bogus, just to avoid the time and stress involved. Third parties paying bills in estates just pay such bills for they can't ascertain the truth easily.

Some persons seek to dominate another, or others by acquiring a boss' position. A person with a poor self image may need to prove to himself or herself he or she does have power over others. Such persons should never be given a position of authority. There are way too many insecure persons in "boss" positions who love the thrill of controlling others.

Karl Rove profiles himself as a superman as he acts like a slave to billionaires, especially David and Charles Koch, who incidentally are the third and fourth richest Americans with $50 billion. With a billion being a thousand million how could anyone logically spend a billion dollars in his adult lifetime? A yacht, a plane, several homes, and plenty to eat. What else is needed in the financial realm?

How many of the world's problems revolve around liars, thieves and the greedy? A person may be a combination of all three. It is also a given the rich have the ability to publicize and twist the truth - or just out and out lie to get the effect they want. Negative ads are well known to be very effective. On today's news Republican Presidential candidate Willard Romney claimed credit for saving the Detroit automotive industry. That is after he very distinctly said, "Let Detroit die!" back when the auto industry was crippled from the President George W. Bush and Republican policies and economy. CNN played several Romney clips from the past which showed without any doubt Romney meant to close Detroit down forever. Commentators were trying to control their laughter at Romney's audacity of claiming to have saved Detroit! Pathetically millions will believe him and vote for such a liar. He made in excess of a quarter billion dollars exporting U. S. jobs and companies, and now he claims he was a savior!

Who gets a fairer trial...a billionaire, or a poor minimum wage earner? It isn't supposed to matter, but we both know it does.

Another well known Republican was also in the business of buying up companies and selling off the valued assets as Romney did. Former U. S. Vice President Dan Quayle also made some quick bucks exporting U. S. jobs and companies. I have been told this is the new way, "so get used to it!" To me being patriotic means assuring our country, The United States of America, remains strong, and that means having jobs and a robust economy here. I just don't understand why Republicans think weakening America is the thing to do. Do Republicans treat their family members the same way, too?

Quayle and his rich Republican associates were in on the purchasing of the "Chrysler Corporation" from Daimler which involved some billions in U. S. tax paid TARP funds. The new company was Cerberus. GMAC, the former financial arm of General Motors, was another company sucking taxpayer funding under Quayle's leadership.

One first step toward a solution to America's problems would be to stop voting for a Dan Quayle, a George W. Bush, a Reagan, a Dan Burton, a Sarah Palin or a Willard Romney. Candidates who are easy puppets are well-liked by rich master puppeteers. A few million dollars in the pocket and a hearty slap on the back, and all is well for the rich!

A change which would resolve so many of our country's problems would be to see every employee receive half the profits he or she generates. There would be no need for food stamps, HEAP or any other emergency support dollars. We all know this isn't going to happen. Employees are set up within a band aid system: struggle, struggle, struggle, go without, then when desperate, go to your family or church; then as a last resort go to the government to get what your employer didn't pay you.

Wages for workers in the past 20 years have increased a total of 18%, but in purchasing power has regressed to the 1980 level. Income for the top 1% has advanced by 300%, a stark difference. Remember, at the same time the top 1% has had the continuous huge Bush tax cuts for 12 years. Those are tax cuts Republicans insist need to become permanent. Never before in our history have we ever had a war without raising taxes. With TWO wars Republicans CUT taxes taking a $5.77 trillion surplus to a $13 trillion debt. Just that sentence alone should set off most sane persons! Have you noticed how Republicans continue with the same drum beat saying this debt is because of President Obama? A trillion dollars a year interest on Bush's debt times 3 years (so far) is $3 trillion.

Replacing the war materials Bush ignored after they were destroyed in the sand, heat and roadside bombs during his terms, cost another two trillion. Bush, Cheney and Rove thought you would be too stupid to understand off the books spending, and leaving the costs of the war for the next President to absorb. You do get it, don't you?

Yes, President Obama did sign for a $787 billion stimulus. In part, it saved all the U. S. businesses which provide parts, tires, etc. to our auto businesses about which Romney said, "Let Detroit die!"

Most of those loans have already been repaid, so most of the Obama stimulus has been repaid already. If you consider unemployment NOT paid, and all the added payroll taxes already collected since Obama's stimulus, it has been a big success.

It put millions back to work after Republicans'/Bush's Great Recession lost millions of jobs and 50,000 U. S. companies in 8 years.
President Obama took over as President Bush was losing almost 800,000 jobs A MONTH in his last month in office. Obama's successes are huge in my mind. If your favorite President had done as well as President Obama has done, would you be happy? He hasn't boasted but he got things done which couldn't get done for over 100 years. He got bin Laden, we're out of Iraq and slated to be out of Afghanistan.

President Obama has been the only President in over 100 years to go after the healthcare issue and get it done. It was an issue he campaigned on and was elected to do. As the issue got bigger and bigger and with costs out in orbit at over 16% of GNP, President Obama got it through without socializing it. All of your medical decisions are being made by you and your doctor; your insurance is still with any insurance carrier you want just as your auto insurance is, and there are added protections like: you can't be dropped or have your premiums raised if you get sick; there are no lifetime or annual limits in payments for your medical care; I believe your plan is portable (you can take it with you;) your children can stay on your policy until age 26; a minimum percentage of the premiums must be spent on patient care; all preventative medical needs are paid 100% without any co-pay; and, pre-existing conditions can't be a reason to refuse a policy to you or charge you higher premiums.

And because everyone must be covered, we, as taxpayers, will no longer get stuck paying for exorbitant emergency room services for those who do not have medical care insurance when they need medical care. Paying $500 or $600 to have an earache checked is ridiculous and expensive; and such things as earaches are predictable. It has been estimated our policy premiums will drop $1017 a year when we don't have to absorb the costs of the uninsured. That alone might allow a vacation, or maybe a new car for you or your family.

Heritage Foundation Individual Healthcare Insurance Mandate
On October 2, 1989, Stuart M. Butler wrote for the right wing Heritage Foundation a position paper regarding healthcare in America, specifically regarding the Individual Mandate. A quote: "a mandate on households certainly would force those with adequate means to obtain insurance protection. Under the Health Plan, there would be such a requirement."

Forms of this plan were introduced in Congress, sometimes with bipartisan support, between 1993 and 2009. Strong backers of this plan included Republicans: Orin Hatch - UT, Robert Bennett - UT, Christopher Bond - MO, and Charles Grassley - IA, among others. Democrats and Republicans joined forces in taking the position people should take personal responsibility for their healthcare costs. No more "free riders!"

The individual mandate is the most debated item. The cure, which Republicans now reject, emanated in October 1989 from their right wing Heritage Foundation owned by the Koch brothers.

The "Health Plan" was also the basis of the Massachusetts' Healthcare Program fought for in detail by Governor Romney who for political reasons now distances himself from it.

Most who analyze why the GOP doesn't support it now, say it has to do with having a Black man in the White House. It is a sad case in this day and age when a large number of people have to die over time for our children to be allowed to fully enjoy their minority friends within a country without racism. Some things only change with time.

General Motors, Chrysler and all their suppliers have been saved. Ford worried its suppliers would fold if GM and Chrysler went under. If that were the case Ford may have failed, too. Millions of jobs have been created and saved.

The grounds were fertile in Northern Africa for democracy to show its buds. Most of our troops are home. The stock market stabilized and went from $7949.09 on January 2009 to $12,868.77 as I make corrections on July 18, 2012. Bin Laden is gone. We've had 27 straight months of jobs and economic improvements replacing jobs Bush lost. What did you expect - magic?

A Republican would crow with such a record! President George W. Bush surely couldn't after his stream of disasters.

We would be doing better than 200,000 to 300,000 job gains each month now if Republicans didn't vote in unison every time to block release of collected fuel and road taxes to be used to repair and expand our highways and bridges. They are in great need of fixing, and such work is commonly acknowledged worldwide as the quickest way to stimulate an economy. Bridges will fail and people will die. I hope your family and I are not the ones. We won't know until it happens. To me not fixing them is insane.

The GOP has stubbornly stuck to its plan of doing whatever is needed to assure President Obama is seen as a failure. For America to fail is o. k. with them as long as they get their way.

I expect Republicans will suddenly come up with the infrastructure idea, chide Democrats for not suggesting it, then release large sums of infrastructure funds just months before the November Presidential election. It's a pattern I have seen them use since I was very young.

If capitalism were allowed to work with all parties involved having equal input without unfair restrictions on workers, it may not be perfect but would come closer to being fair. The employer, the employee and the customer each has input.

Here is a simplified example of a bicycle building factory. If employees want $10 in wages and benefits, the employer makes and delivers a bicycle for $25, plus the $10 in labor, but wants a net profit of $75 (now a total of $110,) and the customer will not pay over $100, someone or more than one has to give up a total of $10. The pressure is usually put on the employees to give in to lower wages and benefits.

You may think I exaggerated the profit side of the example. Not so. It is normal for a fully burdened cost of making and delivering a box of product costing $45 to be sold at a price of $250 to $350 a box. The production costs are reduced even more if that segment of the business is moved to Mexico. Fortune 500 profits would shock you as many of those companies pay as close to minimum wage as possible. Many still pay only $10 to $12 for rigidly screened beginners they easily find in rural areas in America where very reliable employees are abundant.

Having penalties only against employees, and having the government legislate changes to negotiated contracts has no place in capitalism, but it happens every day. A business which squandered employee pension funds resulting in employees losing part or all of their retirement is not right either. I can't think of any penalty aimed at the employer in confrontations between labor and the employer. It's an open invitation to rip off employees.

Employers and businesses hold the money cards which through lobbying and donations get the laws which etch away at the rights of working people. When labor pools its money to fight back, those who hate labor complain relentlessly. They are not accustomed to equality or pushback and seemingly don't know there are no profits without employees.

A business needs an idea, sufficient investment, leadership, a facility, raw materials, a distributions system and customers with enough wealth who are willing to pay a price all can live with for the product or service offered. Even if all these were available, nothing would be produced or sold without employees, unless one works alone, or with one or more partners.

Often a potential business operator with a great idea doesn't have adequate funding and for whatever reason(s) can't raise it anywhere. Government backed loans like SBA loans (Small Business Administration) fill the bill and a business is born. The business then repays the debt with monthly payments to a bank selected. Counties often set aside a lump of money to loan directly to similar businesses setting up within that county. Again, there is a repayment schedule. As the funds are returned more loans can be shuffled out.

Troubles begin when sleazy operators go into such loans knowing how to game the system. Too often a business repays little or nothing, goes bankrupt, then ends up buying the same business setup for around 10 cents on the dollar. Having kept all the money possible, he or she then has the cash which can be used to buy stuff back at auction.

In 1964, with 10 brand new dump trucks a man was able to get a significant 24 hour a day trucking contract. Hired trucks were not paid until they complained they had no fuel money. The trucking contractor claimed he wasn't being paid by the main contractor but as a good fellow he'd give truckers money from his personal funds, at least enough for fuel.

The bank demanded payments and he stiffed them for months then gave them drips and drabs. He pulled that off for the whole construction season taking in mountains of money which disappeared. His trucks were not maintained with even normal maintenance. In late fall when the bank took the trucks from him he filed bankruptcy owing the bank, truckers, fuel companies and everyone who fell for his line of promises. He walked away with a fortune and a smile. In my opinion it was a calculated bankruptcy from the beginning. Apparently, bankers and others didn't do their jobs; unless it was an inside job in which directors of thrift banks loaned money to family members or themselves without ever making a payment.

The thrift bank deal cost Americans $125 billion or more. No monies were ever recovered. Recovery was blocked by their father, I mean a U. S. President. Such loan losses are just quietly paid for from our tax dollars.

States and counties are so desperate for businesses with jobs to move to their locations, they end up bidding taxpayer dollars offering to buy expensive prime business land, build a state of the art building with lighting, parking lots, natural gas, a new electric supply, water, roadways, railroad sidings - and on and on. On top of that there is a 10 year break from paying any property taxes. States and the federal government often throw in tax credits to sweeten the deal even more. This is not capitalism or free enterprise!!!! It is socialism for corporations!!

From memory I can recall such massive projects in southern states where numerous brand new auto plants were built. The reasoning behind many of these corporate welfare programs may be based on good thinking, but there is no end to it. Every day I read about more of our money given to profitable corporations.

Today's front page of "The Daily Star" spoke of $365 million for a chip lab at the State University College of Nanoscale Science and Engineering at Albany, N. Y. Companies benefiting directly are IBM, Samsung and Global Foundries. In the grand scheme of things such shots of support start to add up after a while! On page 10 the story reminds us for the third year we taxpayers will continue to work toward dredging the remaining 2 million cubic yards of sediment from the Hudson River put there by General Electric. It is taking more than a billion dollars from the Superfund to remove the PCB's (poly-biphenyls.) Using the same Republican laws Romney used General Electric pays NO U. S. taxes even though it operates within the U. S., sells to the U. S. government, and continuously uses our country's infrastructure.

Earlier I wrote a list of about 150 topics you may want to think about. Number 43 gives a list of some of the corporate welfare items so prevalent in the U. S.

News of Stafford college student loans also occupies space today in the Daily Star." Here is how the money flow works for the most part.

1. Banks borrow money from the federal government (us) for one quarter of 1% or from you in a savings account.

2. With the backing of our government, banks loan those dollars to students for 6.8% interest, half (3.4%) of which is paid by taxpayers. The taxpayer amount is $6 billion a year. Banks have little time or expense involved, and NO RISK, for we 100% guarantee those loans. There is no reason for a lending institution to do any checking on those borrowing, so in effect this is a $12 billion boondoggle for bankers who are rich and Republican. Are you beginning to see the pattern?

I am not making a negative judgment about helping our population become well educated, for education benefits all or us. We would not have phones, calculators, computers or automobiles if the inventors didn't have the necessary education to do the thinking and planning involved. Just for clarity, all education is not just technology stuff either.

For just a moment let's say government is an integral part in education, and using basic logic, wouldn't it be more beneficial to the students and the taxpayers to just loan money directly to the students at one quarter percent and skip the other $12 billion which ends up in bankers' hands for basically nothing? Taxpayers would be $6 billion ahead each year, and students would have a $6 billion interest advantage each year meaning it would save them $12 billion a year starting 7/01/12; even more when you consider compounding.

Is that thinking too logical and simple? It seems like a no-brainer. But that is not allowed by Republicans! It is not in sync with the GOP plan to always make money drift to the rich. To me that is not Christian, fair, logical or necessary! It gives the rich unfair, unneeded enrichment while taking from those who are earnestly trying to become educated in their efforts to improve the lives of many.

3. Repayment is required - always.

4. On July 1, 2012, if the bill is not passed and signed, the interest rate charged directly to the student will be 6.8% and their total interest would become $12 billion, but as always the bank will have no risk if a student should default. A Congressional bill passed by President Obama would allow a continuation of the program as it currently exists. Republicans are insisting on paying for the $6 billion by taking it from Social Security.

WHY CAN'T REPUBLICANS UNDERSTAND SOCIAL SECURITY AND MEDICARE DOLLARS ARE TAXED DOLLARS TAKEN FROM AND BELONGING TO EMPLOYEES, AMERICAN WORKERS? THESE ARE NOT GENERAL FUND DOLLARS. WE EARNED AND SAVED THESE DOLLARS WITH NO HELP FROM YOU! KEEP YOUR PATHETIC GREEDY HANDS OFF!

I hope if a person makes it to one of the two houses of Congress, he or she has enough brain power to know these are not general fund or budget dollars. That means those who do continue to take from the retirement dollars of

America's workers are showing a very unbecoming, greedy, arrogant style! Social Security and Medicare Fund monies should not be shown as a part of our national budget. We do not show monies the IRS has in its custody belonging to citizens when the national budget is formulated. The IRS returns the monies it has as its regulations allow. Social Security and Medicare funds are not much different.

It's easy to be reckless with monies in programs they despise. The lacking of funding is the biggest argument Republicans use when saying, "Social Security and Medicare can't work! There is no money!" Of course not! They stole all of it with no intention of repaying it! Multiple trillions! They do this to older Americans who built and paid for the development of this country, fought its wars, sacrificed in other ways and put their money into Social Security and Medicare.

Shame on those who steal from those who have been counting on getting the return of their own already taxed dollars now they are nearing or in retirement. Is there some sick humor in jerking them (us) around?

If America is taken over by a fascist dictator, you can instantly say good-bye to your Social Security and Medicare. Poof! The rightwing hates them with a passion!

They disregard the truth scaring citizens on purpose, something I find very repulsive. If they succeed, it becomes a means of left handedly tax shifting an even higher burden onto America's hard workers; and it is pure theft. With relative deprivation the rich escape paying while the poorer pay more.

I have mixed feelings about taxpayers shelling out $6 billion. Direct loans to students could have been given at one quarter of 1% with a savings of $6 billion to us; and $6 billions to students. Republicans would fight the $6 billion loss they would encounter. The student loans represent a figure greater than all credit card balances combined.

Major banks are set up with many heavy investors receiving wild pay and benefits for no show positions. Those with preferred stocks are guaranteed special rights. With the W. Bush/Paulson bailout, stock holders in major banks, even foreign banks, were effectively made whole financially from huge losses. That wasn't the same for everyone except for the crooks of banks, Wall St. and insurance companies like AIG which received $180 billion of our money.

Who should pay for college is a debatable issue, too. In a perfect world an employee would be justly compensated which would take into account the time and costs involved in becoming an employee with needed skills. If it worked that way many students with great potential likely would never sit in college classrooms. Without doubt education in general raises the standard of living for everyone. Too many employers do not come even close to paying for one's time and expenses in college.

College is a grueling, stressful life punctuated with times when steam is let go. Long times spent studying for tests or in writing a term paper for a perfectionist professor wrecks one's health in terms of sleeping and eating properly. All-nighters and coffee can wind you up and dump you in a heap! Working at a job usually is easier than college.

From time to time individuals come up with solutions. Some are great, some so-so and others have been tried over and over with results which a sixth grader could tell you don't work. Trickle down economics has been pushed by Republicans for 3 decades. The Great Recession is total proof of what it does to people and a country's economy.

Every day billions of our treasury are dispensed to corporations, and to individuals. With individuals there is usually urgency in the need for medical care, food or other basic needs. Much of what is given corporations is offered in a competitive way to encourage a business to locate somewhere, or from a Republican majority setting up a giveaway to a company which has lobbied it, or has indicated it will donate to them. The money is looked at as so many more gallons of salt water from an ocean, there free for the taking. There is pretty much an unlimited supply available with no consideration to consequences. It is evident to most people this system can't continue as our country fights wars and everything else on borrowed money, and while cutting taxes mainly on the rich for twelve years. Add to that the dramatic drop of the highest federal income tax bracket, in the past 40 years, from 91% down to effective rates of 13.9% or even less.

Chapter 6 SEVERAL POSSIBLE SOLUTIONS

My SOLUTIONS are quite simple!

1.   Any form of welfare given a business or an individual is A LOAN with an interest rate equal to the rate the government loans money to banks, currently one quarter percent. Helping individuals, families and businesses can be a good thing. If a business is viable enough to continue it should be able to repay the loan. If not it should fail now before vacuuming taxpayer earned money into a black hole in which scammers can carefully skim the loot. The rules should be carefully written to prevent the business from avoiding repayment. Let's have 1200 pages, not 3 as Bush and Paulson suggested on handing out $700 BILLION under TARP. With 1200 pages of rules, the purpose of Affordable Care Act can be carried out. Three pages under TARP had no restrictions on what was supposed to be help for small businesses and home owners in trouble. None of the money went to them.

For an individual whose family is in desperate straits there would be gratitude for being able to get "an advance" on future earnings. Flexibility could keep a compassionate aura over the loan allowing repayment on an ability level. A contract should be signed in advance in which all the rules are understood. A windfall income like winning the lottery would necessitate an immediate full repayment. HEAP, WIC, food stamps and such would all become part of the same "bill" which would encumber both a husband and wife or any other household persons helped by the loan(s.)

In one or two generations all citizens would likely lose the entitlement attitude. People could have pride in being able to care for themselves and their family unit while still having the comfort of knowing loans could be available during hard times which befall too many.

Of course, there will be some who will never be able to repay the loans, but compared with now when nobody repays, it would be a great gain. Knowing repayment with interest is required would likely shorten the time duration and possibly lower the amount of each monthly loan. Of course, a time duration, as in welfare support, should be involved as is the case now. I believe there is a 2 year limit on welfare. Bill Clinton ran for President with that as one of his pillars - and he was able to put it into law. It saved lots of money.

If initiated it must follow a path of few exceptions. A profitable corporation can't claim, "If you make us repay we'll lose our stockholders." That would be like admitting they can't survive without welfare.

Republican voters, who are also stuck with high gasoline and heating prices every day, just ignore it when Republicans, in unison, vote to continue enormous subsidies to companies which are the largest and most profitable in the world. Where are their minds? Logic disappears! Enough of the corporate welfare! Get a brain - - and a backbone! Other left-handed corporate welfare must be avoided, too.

Much of such corporate welfare is given by states along with donations from federal funds. It would work much better if states were required to go along with this program, but I do believe in states' rights. Holding back on related federal funds, as the federal government currently does to keep states in line with the 55 miles per hour speed limit, could be used to push cooperation.

With most of those funds being repaid, taxes would be less allowing lower tax rates on both businesses and individuals. All of us need many government services which we could not possibly provide on our own. Roads, schools, airports, government buildings, military strength... along with thousands of other services are costly, but well worth it. Without agencies to keep everything flowing well, we would quickly be under the control of a dictator. Thousands of years of history prove that.

Next, in no particular order, are a few more solutions to help America's corporations and citizens.

2.   Energy is a finite resource. During WWII Japan's oil products were being cut off. That is why Japan attacked Pearl Harbor in Hawaii where much of the U. S. Pacific Fleet was harbored. Those ships would be the ones preventing deliveries to Japan.

With no energy, businesses can't be run so one's economy will fizzle and fail fast. It takes a huge amount of energy to power airplanes, tanks, ships and for generating electricity; and let's not forget heating and cooling our homes. Japan would have been a sitting duck ready for takeover for it has no energy source of its own I am aware of.

Republicans pushed and pushed for drilling on lands we taxpayers own in Alaska. Now almost all that production is shipped to China, the largest Communist country; Japan; Korea, and elsewhere where it is used to power machinery which had been installed in U. S. factories supplying Americans jobs. Thanks to Romney, Dan Quayle and W. Bush those jobs are no longer in America. More than 50,000 U. S. factories shipped their machinery overseas between 2001 and January 2009.

Did drilling in Alaska bring down U. S. gasoline prices? NO! Republicans continue to push for more Alaskan oil drilling under the same conditions. British Petroleum isn't even a U. S. company, nor is it a responsible company. On t. v. ads, it boasts it has appropriated $20 billion for people along the Gulf of Mexico, people whose lives were crushed by an idiotic spill which could have easily, with a few dollars, been prevented. Appropriated, maybe yes; released to victims - not so much! Only a small portion. It's not what you do; it's about how good your PR is. How much would it have cost to buy a battery to put into a strategic piece of monitoring equipment to help prevent a spill? Sloppy work produces disasters.

U. S. coal is exported every day to China to pollute the same atmosphere as ours. Each week China has a new coal fired electric plant come on line to meet its rapidly growing needs. If the coal is going to be burned on this planet, it might as well be burned here in the U. S. By saying that, I am not encouraging it. The associated problems are real and need to be dealt with.

In order to get citizens to go along with tapping the Northeast's 5 natural gas strata, the largest being the Marcellus Shale, drilling companies have claimed it would supply all Americans with energy for over 100 years.

Would it surprise you to know the first recent Northeast pipelines were built to NYC and New Jersey ports for exporting? Natural gas had been at prices up to almost $16 per MMBTU (million British Thermal Units.) Now it is $2.25 because of the glut after many wells were drilled in Pennsylvania and New York State, yet it is NOT being made available to us here where it is being produced. Our local electric and gas provider, now owned by a company from Spain, told me a few years ago it has no plans to sell natural gas to residents of my town or village. Their closest line is about 4 miles away.

In NYS drillers are required to pay at least 12.5% of the value of the natural gas to the land owners. Drillers sell to subsidiaries which then sell to India, China or elsewhere for $6 to $8 or more. The land owners gets 12.5% of the $2.25 not the $6 or $8. Greed abounds. Natural gas, at those prices, would help cut my heating bill drastically. Propane is a derivative of natural gas. My propane price has gone up over 10% in the past year despite wholesale prices crashing.

Several drilling advocates have been brazen enough to say, "There has never been a spill or leak of the carcinogenic chemicals used in fracking. It would take a book to tell about all of them. Last week a truck driver emptied the tractor trailer load of mud water onto a farmer's field; and was caught. Lots of hydrochloric acid was just reported spilled at a drill site. They have used the water for dust control on their dirt roads.

Reports to the government are super vague and cannot be used to figure where the millions of gallons of contaminated water per well have gone. States don't appear to be very interested in regulating on a better level. On the local level there are strong verbal fights every day over the possible contamination of our land and water.

About 60 miles south of me along I-88 and near the Susquehanna River a well was drilled. Now natural gas boils up through the waters in the Susquehanna about 2 miles away. In Pennsylvania residents can hold a match next to their water faucets and witness a natural gas fire as the faucet is turned on.

Those pushing for drilling are almost 100% Republican from my observations. Truth does not get in the way of good stories with the drillers and their representatives. Even if a person were somewhat open minded about drilling he can't believe or trust them. Anything to save money is a good thing! In the ads on television they say the wells are protected by concrete and steel. Many people know salt can dissolve both concrete and steel, so what is the point? Most of NYS was once under the ocean, and has left a lot of salt deposits throughout the earth's crust, as in Syracuse where salt mines are large enough to put a school building in. History has proven the wells leak.

Knowing it isn't true, Republicans have blamed President Obama for stopping the Keystone Pipeline from Canada to Texas and New Orleans. Republican governors are the ones who put temporary holds on the pipeline because they rightfully were worried about their states' water supplies. Each state has the absolute control over what and where pipelines are built within the state. And those Republicans who blubber on with false stories saying "Obama is holding up the pipeline!" are full of it and they know it. Shame on them! And shame on news' "journalists" who don't call them out on such lies!

The sad thing is the GOP sticks to a story once a "leader" tells it even if the truth is exposed. People do believe a story if they hear it enough times regardless of its truthfulness. They should learn to question the source especially when a pattern emerges.

The ports in New Orleans and Texas already are exporting oil, gasoline and natural gas. If the U. S. continues to export our oil supplies, our coal and our natural gas resources, what will be left for America? What will American citizens have to use in seventy-five years; 200 years, or 1000 years from now? They may have some unkind words for us when they sit there in "WaterWorld."

Exxon Mobil makes tens of billions in profits each quarter as it exports every gallon of oil it can find here in the U. S. A. If there is no pride, laws are the only way to reserve OUR energy. If not on private land, let's at least take steps to not export energy from public lands owned by the citizens of our country. Are we stupid???? A country with little or no energy is not a world power. We'd be a sitting duck like Japan if we give up all our energy. We can't run tanks, fighter jets and transport vehicles with windmills and solar power! Would someone get a grip?

The oil from Canada and from the Balkans in our northwestern states is to be exported eventually after the Keystone Pipeline gets it delivered to southern refineries in Texas and Louisiana.

How about our Alaskan oil going to our west coast, Gulf oil supplying our south, and a pipeline supplying Canadian and Balkan oil to a new refinery between Chicago and Buffalo for use in the Northeast along with the natural gas. New Jersey has refineries along with some others along our EastCoast. Where needed tanker ships can transport crude via The Great Lakes and the St. Lawrence River to New Jersey's refineries if pipeline access is missing.

We need to start thinking about America, especially when people like Romney, Quayle and W. Bush are selling us out for the biggest buck! Doesn't anybody else feel the same way? Sometimes like after the 2010 election, I feel so alone. You can't want different and stay home during elections. If you do, you will get different, for sure.

3.   Let there be no wars without it being properly declared - as it already stands on the books.

4.   Let there be automatic rejection (without the need of Congress' approval) of off-the-books spending as W. Bush did repeatedly to make his

budgets look better historically. Off-the-books spending is for unforeseen matters which are to last only a month or two. Wars lasting over 6 years are not emergencies and need to be in the regular budget. The calling of it by one Congressman or Senator should be all that is needed. A party in the majority could not block the legal path as they do. If off-the-books spending is done, it should be added to the regular budget with an asterisk. Records are kept to show truth.

5.   Do not continue to give government contracts to criminal corporations or individuals. War contractors steal from us as a matter of everyday business. Candidates should have the backbone to expose an opponent for illegal things that candidate has done. It was known that when Dick Cheney was CEO of Halliburton, a U. S. company, he continuously broke U. S. laws by selling oil drilling equipment and services to Hussein in Iraq. As he left Halliburton after nominating himself into the Vice Presidential slot, he was given an $18 million thank you present from them. Halliburton has since moved its business headquarters to the unconstricted Middle East country of Dubai, and I believe no longer pays taxes to the U. S., its biggest customer.

When I served, we were reminded constantly if we went AWOL over 30 days we would be charged as a deserter; and would spend at least 7 years in the stockades in Ft. Leavenworth. A candidate AWOL two or three years is not Presidential by any standard. Shame on America for allowing it! It minimizes the service of every troop who followed the rules, regulations and laws without deserting his unit. A deserter should not be glorified or allowed to become our President.

6.   Rewrite whatever regulations are necessary so the income of hedge fund persons is taxable as regular income. For comparison sake, in the midst of 8% real inflation (a guess on my part,) I will have to pay taxes on one quarter percent interest I am receiving as income from a portion of my retirement...a large loss in purchasing power. Several hedge fund managers earn over a billion dollars each year - and pay no taxes. A couple of them make over 2 billion each a year. Republicans dig in and fight all efforts Democrats make to have such income taxed. Can you spell "ridiculous?"

7.   Allow persons with interest income to deduct a real cost of living increase before showing interest as income on tax forms.

8.   Charge persons or businesses when they use a government facility like a canal. Yacht owners and ocean going vessels should pay to use The Erie Canal. The costs shouldn't be passed on to NYS Thruway users.

9.   Communication should be encouraged. There should be no tax or fees associated with communication. Phone taxes were put on phone

bills during WWII as another revenue burden on citizens who were paying through the nose in every way already. It's time they go!

10.   Require hedge fund traders to put forth real money for their investment trades instead of allowing the use of massive amounts of imaginary money to invest. The Koch brothers are examples of those who control the prices of gasoline, heating fuel and many other items by manipulation through hedge funds. They have $50 billion but only have to put up pennies as they manipulate many aspects of the market. It gives them a magnified amount of clout in market influence. Their impact greatly affects every U. S. family.

11.   Take away all or most of the advantages businesses have when they use and abuse the United States Postal Service. A long cardboard tube with a metal key in it won't fit into most mailboxes. Such had to be treated as packages meaning the vehicle had to be shut down and secured, then the package had to be taken to the door. It cost the business 5 cents. It would cost anyone else $5 or more. When I worked for the Post Office I delivered hundreds of those tubes. In one case I had to go to the patron's door three days in a row. That is a lot of service for 5 cents - and is very unfair to all the customers who pay regular charges for such mail. Enough of the ridiculous, unfair corporate welfare which hurts the USPS. Something like 70% of the mail...(BBM) bulk business mail/junk mail... brings in about 25% of the revenue or less. Businesses should carry their own weight without cost-shifting.

12.   Come forth with a 50 word or less universal agreement for using a program such as one on the computer.

13.   Let free enterprise work with the sale and movement of medicines allowing price negotiations as done in the Veterans' Administration, thereby saving 50 to 70%. Republicans fought and fought that setup when it came to Medicare drugs. How can anyone see that as anything else but billions in unneeded extra profits for the pharmaceuticals protected by Congressional Republicans who say they believe in free enterprise?

14.   Have our government do regular checks on drugs to assure they are what they say they are; they are sterile and safe, and they have the correct strength labeled. China, where a large shares of U. S. medicine components are made, is not really a reliable source on many items. Now Russia is equaling China's status.

15.   Tax U. S. companies uniformly. All companies (GE and Romney's, too) should pay U. S. taxes.

16. Do away with phony non-profits; and take away the tax free status of "churches" which act as political organizations. Also, take away the non-profit status of Blue Cross/Blue Shield and all such profit generators.

17. Make outfits collecting money for Veterans or such organizations, register and make monthly reports which the government should post online. The reports need to show what was paid to the 100 highest paid employees or officers, and how much went to Veterans, children, medical research, etc. The requirements should be very detailed and specific. Add criminal teeth.

A NYC outfit collected $60 million in the past 3 years for U. S. Veterans. According to news on television not even 10 cents has gone to Veterans in any way. It is stealing, pathetic and very wrong making collections for good purposes much more unlikely. Real providers need to expose the horrible ones. And how high are the benefits and pay at the "good" outfits? They don't publicize such very well either. Require a minimum amount like 95% as an amount which must go directly to Veterans or other named "beneficiaries." Prohibit abusers from being able to collect for any organization again. Our laws are so weak they invite criminal minds to start turning. Social Security funds are dispersed for less than one half of 1%.

I know capitalizing the V in Veterans is not correct grammar, but I always do it out of personal respect, and without an apology.

18. Require ministers, "churches" and any organization collecting donations on a more massive scale to post online dollars received, a full disclosure of exactly where the money goes, and the personal wealth of those asking for the donations. Religion is used to make many, many ministers, wealthy with tens and hundreds of millions of dollars in personal wealth from donations intended to help the poor, sick and such. They should not object to putting forth particulars of their personal wealth since they are asking for money. Many politicians take the opportunities to hang out publicly with ministers who I see as money grubbing thieves. They often take right wing stances which appear to me to be opposite of what Jesus taught. With little effort they can become very wealthy with some ending up in jail. In my opinion people are way too trusting. This is not intended to offend or put down most ministers who do lots of good while receiving low pay. The bad few should be quickly exposed. Stop giving them your wealth!

19. The codes written for public building construction need heavy revisions, the sooner the better. Most two story public buildings could be 3 stories in the same space. The costs to build, maintain along with the costs of heating and cooling could be drastically lower. And as put forth earlier, the need to replace fresh air at such a voluminous rate defies common sense. School buildings have a heater with a blower

which runs almost continuously drawing in frigid air to replace oxygen in each room. Oxygen represents 20% of air. Our red blood cells capture only a tiny portion of that 20% with each breath. The same energy and cost savings can be saved in every store, mall or other public building, too. The total effect overall could be huge.

20.   People need to change the mindset regarding concrete and steel buildings being good only 14 or 30 years. Tons of explosives are needed to bring down some tough buildings and stadiums, which were probably built with tax dollars - and likely are being replaced by another building or stadium paid for by taxpayers. Locally, a high rise parking garage maybe 30 years old is being talked about in terms of replacement. Concrete parking garages, or expensive eight foot concrete flower pots can be treated with a water seal sold everywhere. Hydraulic cement can replace any concrete which has failed. Does NYC, Tokyo or London replace its concrete buildings every 25 to 50 years? Some are over 100 years old and doing well. We are a planet with limited resources. Too many don't put that fact into their everyday thinking.

21.   When the need is there to build and maintain highways within a state or within the U. S., legislators should look around and think: 1) how much money do we need for this project, and who should pay for it? I like that concept. Those who use something should be the ones to pay for it.

In NYS gambling with LOTTO, and other such games was set forth as a means of adding to the regular funding dollars for K-12 education, allocations above and beyond the norm. Little is given to those winning ticket holders. Where does the rest go?

During slower economic times, as in Bush's Great Recession when businesses need a boost in sales and workers need jobs, the norm is to pick up the pace in spending those collected fuel, gasoline and road taxes. Whether in Europe, Asia or in the U. S., it has been a universally accepted no-brainer decision.

Republicans and Democrats have always been in unison when the economy dictates a need for stimulation, that is, until Barack Obama was elected President. At the opening of the first day Congress resumed with Senate Minority Leader Mitch McConnell declaring their number one priority for the next four years was to assure Barack Obama, our first Black President, was to remain a one term President. Not the economy, or the two wars, or poverty or jobs; let's assure that Black man doesn't get a second term! Despite common sense, or how each of us would be effected, Republicans would rather see our economy and country fail than to take a chance a Black Democrat would be re-elected. In my 70+ years I don't recall this ever happening before. It is pathetic and sad. In all honesty Republicans have hurt me and other Americans far more than the totality of all what foreign terrorists have done to us. I implore you to do everything you can, especially in voting, to rid our country's leadership from such prejudiced, uncaring Congressmen and Senators. They literally sickened me. As I read and studied what they purposefully did to America, I had to stop researching and writing for two months. Now behind the gun I am working in haste to get this book out there in enough time before November's election.

Right wingers do not want to admit they took those tax revenues and paid toward useless, unneeded wars which were planned back in **1997** in The Project of the New American Century. Google it.

In **1997** a large group of right wing Republicans was quite vocal about invading Iraq, the same country Dick Cheney was selling oil field materials and services to despite a U. S. embargo against it. It is the same type of restriction we presently have against Iran and North Korea. There are pictures out there of Cheney and Rumsfeld in Iraq smiling as they were giving Saddam Hussein vigorous handshakes.

There were hundreds of billions of dollars worth of oil there, pretty much for the taking. Hussein already had about $30 billion in U. S. currency hidden in a sealed brick home I would guess ready to throw into an airplane in the event he had to depart in a hurry.

Oil was so prominent in their minds that during the 2003 Thunder and Awe Iraq invasion President W. Bush had a decision to make. A warehouse was discovered full with over a dozen tractor trailer loads of powerful C-2 explosives which Hussein's forces were preparing to take. The Decider ordered all troops to go protect the oil wells and pipelines instead of guarding the warehouse. For nine years afterwards our troops have been killed and maimed by crude homemade roadside bombs planted in roads our troops used. It is believed the bombs were made from the C-2 explosives originally housed within that warehouse. It could also have been used in many other destructive acts around the world since then. C-2 is light in weight and VERY powerful.

You may have voted for a person who was more concerned for money from oil than for the lives of your son or daughter, husband, niece, nephew, uncle, father or family friend. Your votes have consequences. Some brains or genes are apparently wired for greed instead of caring for life. The choice to save "the oil" was said to have been a quick one.

After Bush was appointed President by 5 of the only 9 people who are above the law, he made appointments as Presidents do. See how many names you recognize who were so deliberate in concocting stories for the invasion. This is only a partial list of members of The Project of the New American Century in **1997**, a right wing D. C. "think tank" aimed at keeping and increasing "U. S. dominance and pre-eminence," while engaging "in simultaneous major theater wars."

Special Assistant to the President, Elliot Abrams; Under Secretary of State, Richard Armitage (the same person who leaked Secret Agent Valerie Plame's identity, an act of treason;) Under Secretary of State/U. S. Ambassador John R. Bolton; Vice President Richard Cheney; Defense Policy Advisory Board Eliot A. Cohen; Director International Broadcasting Bureau

Seth Cropsey; Under Secretary of State Global Affairs Paula Dobriansky; Department Assistant for National Security Affairs Aaron Friedberg; President Council on Bioethics Francis Fukuyama; U. S. Ambassador to Afghanistan Zalmay Khalilzad; Chief of Staff U. S. Vice President I. Lewis "Scooter" Libby; Assistant Secretary of Defense Peter W. Rodman; Secretary of Defense Donald Rumsfeld; NATO Randy Scheunemann; Deputy Secretary of Defense and president of The World Bank Paul Wolfowitz; Department of Defense Comptroller Dov S. Zakheim; Office U. S. Trade Representative and president of The World Bank Robert B. Zoellick.

Additional original PNAC members: William Kristol; John McCain; Ellen Bork; J. Danforth Quayle; Gary Bauer; Robert Kagen; Donald Kagen; Bruce Jackson; Mark Gerson; Gary Schmitt; Michael Goldfarb; William J. Bennett; Jean Kilpatrick; Richard Lowry; Hillel Fradkin; William Schneider, Jr.; Robert Zoellick; Rich Shultz; Stephen Kantany; Charles Krauthammer; Steven Rosen, and Jeb Bush.

After reading these names, and going online to read more, wouldn't you be surprised if the Republican majority **didn't** take us into multiple Mid-Eastern wars?? **Do these names give you a sense about who was really running our government?**

The security information said to be from England was nothing more than a lame excuse to spend $4 TRILLION, kill over 5000 innocent, young American boys and girls, and maim around 50,000 troops who now must beg for help which they don't receive when they return to America alive. President Bush quietly cut billions from monies for Veterans on the very day he invaded the Middle East. How any Veteran would vote for him defies any logic. Republicans can compete because they have their followers revved up on various issues (The Flag/patriotism, abortion and religion) with some believing those continuous streams of lies. Proven false stories are still being circulated by military members on Facebook. Please correct those who continue such lies, lies which make Veterans feel some don't support them. We Democrats demand our government takes care of our Veterans as heroes who deserve the best care possible! And immediately. If you are a Veteran who has given up some of your hopes, please know we want you to get help right now, and that we love and appreciate you. Let's make noise together and get the help you and your family deserve. Don't give up. None of this is your fault.

There still exists hatred for Clinton lying over a personal matter, while calling Reagan a hero after he arrogantly lied to us repeatedly over our national security in the Iran/Contra deal. Ask a Republican to explain that divergence in thought to you. What Reagan did was treasonous, pure and simple; and our country has provisions for dealing with treason. Those provisions don't include worshipping him.

Needed highway and bridge construction and repair are desperately needed - now, but the party of "NO" stubbornly stands in unison against it.

When you vote or make donations don't reward them for putting us into danger and keeping our economy down. Let's use those taxes collected from gasoline and road use to fix our roads and bridges as quickly as possible and save lives. Tell Republicans you are fed up with their childish actions. Elect only Democrats!

22.   Royalties on public land resources like oil and natural gas have been set way too low. Additionally, W. Bush told agencies to leave such producers alone, and not collect royalties. He even exempted drillers from the Clean Water Act leaving them to a wild West scenario. Does that sound like he represented citizens? Or Corporations? There is a big difference! As BP, a foreign company, took our oil free, it also messed with our southern coastal states in a big way.

BP and Exxon both had a hand in the Alaskan oil which was spilled 22 years ago from the Valdez. To date no payment for the cleanup has been made to our country. Royalties should be high to go along with $108 a barrel oil. Royalty charges were likely set before a barrel of oil was $22 when W. Bush was appointed President in 2000.

23.   Especially with countries which add import taxes to our exports, we need to reciprocate with our own tariffs on their products. China has been well known for currency manipulation which hurts Americans. If we simply meet their abuses with counter actions, things would get resolved, and we wouldn't look so wimpy and stupid.

Chapter 7 MEET SOME REPUBLICANS

Michele Bachmann

When I think of right wing Republicans many names flash through my mind. Michele Bachmann was running as a GOP Presidential candidate against President Obama recently. She showed no shame as she continued with lies and deceit. On a Sunday A. M. show (6-27-11) Bachmann was asked by the interviewer why she continued saying "President Obama issued only one drilling permit in the Gulf since elected President," when in fact over 300 had been issued. She refused to answer. She was using that story as a means of getting campaign donations at a time gasoline was creeping over $4.00 again.

It is well known negative ads and lies work well in politics. Throw in the Flag, some religion, derogatory inferences against minorities, and racism in code, and insecure people are riled up and ready to fight. I am old enough to remember daily racist jokes against Polish, Blacks, Spanish and Italians. As they put others down they felt taller and superior.

Bachmann regularly elevated herself as an expert in taxes which, by extension, would make her an "expert in restoring the economy." She had handled ONE tax case as an attorney according to news reports. That made her an expert. She might have had more credibility if she had voted for or proposed at least one bill designed to help our economy grow.

She railed against subsidies and was caught off guard when asked why she and her psychologist PHD Doctor husband, Marcus, received farm subsidies in excess of $260,000, $24,000 in staff training subsidies for Bachmann and Associates in Lake Elmo, and over $137,000 from Medicaid. Nobody voiced opposition to Medicaid more than Michele. She is the perfect example of a Republican! She instantly denied receiving the farm subsidies which made the questioner ask why she had declared it on a required income form for Congress. Again, no answer.

Her husband had also received vast amounts of government funds when he saw patients thereby taking from the government udder. A specialty of his was to change gay people to straight.

And how could they host twenty-two farm workers, oops, I mean foster children, when both she and her husband were so busy with their careers?

Prescott S. Bush

The Bush family has such a history. I continue to be astounded and even frightened as I find more of what has taken place in that family. Actual evidence exists.

Senator Prescott S. Bush was father of President George Herbert Walker Bush, and grandfather to President George W. Bush.

Senator Prescott S. Bush was at least twice notified by our government to stop selling war materials to Hitler, materials which could be used to kill American troops. According to what I read any person can actually read those notices online by using Google.

Prescott was the son of Samuel Prescott Bush, a federal government official in charge of coordinating major weapons' contractors in WWI. Prescott married George Herbert Walker's daughter. In 1924, Mr. Walker, a very wealthy, well known St. Louis investment banker, wanted the best for his daughter so he set up a new investment company putting his son-in-law, Prescott, in as one of the directors. Union Banking Corporation was mainly owned and operated by a very wealthy German industrialist who, as early as 1921, not only was fascinated by Adolf Hitler, he wrote Hitler's autobiography and donated huge amounts of money to Hitler's efforts including buying a Munich palace which was to become Hitler's headquarters.

Fritz Thyssen also owned Brown Brothers Harriman. Prescott was a director and part owner in both companies which eventually set up the Bush family fortune and political dynasty. Republicans had run the U. S. economy, with a heavy fascist flavor instead of democracy, into the Great Depression. The result was the stock market crashed in 1929.

People were crushed to lose everything. Many committed suicide while the Mellons, Rockefellers and others became very rich.

Republicans lost favor causing a resounding Democratic win for the Presidency and both houses of Congress. Franklin Delano Roosevelt was President and Democrats now controlled Congress. Right wing fascist Republicans wanted workers and regular people to have nothing, with all rights going to corporations the same as in Germany and Italy. When FDR came out with the New Deal, corporate leaders and stock holders went bonkers. Back then, very few people owned stocks. There were no 401-K's or such. Many Republicans had actually supported Germany during WWI. Within 100 days of FDR's election a secret organization, the American Liberty League, was formed by several rich corporate and Wall St. persons to form a coup to rid America of democracy, and replace it with a fascist dictatorship patterned after Hitler and Mussolini's. Names of those belonging to ALL included Prescott S. Bush, DuPont, General Foods, U. S. Steel, Grayson Murphy, and J. P. Morgan. Like Hitler their thoughts were like KKK members according to lengthy writings online.

Also shown are pictures and actual scenes and speeches. One picture showed George H. W. Bush wearing a Nazi military dress hat, maybe the entire uniform. Another speech shows Arnold Swartzenegger praising Hitler. Arnold's father was a Nazi. Unbelievably, Californians voted for him. One article compared Karl Rove, George W.'s "brain," to Hitler's advisor, Joseph Gerbel.

The ALL group was led by Prescott S. Bush. The plan was to overthrow FDR with 500,000 rogue WWI U. S. troops, unhappy with their lackluster treatment after coming home. With brute force they were to topple FDR forcing him to stay there as a powerless figurehead.

Republican Senator Heinz's family, along with Colgate, Birds Eye and General Motors were in. Prescott would explain to all Roosevelt wasn't doing well health wise, and because of that he would have a super secretary to help. The super secretary would secretly be the dictator. Should war break out again in Europe the American Liberty League was to steer the U. S. into joining and supporting Adolf Hitler.

For some reason much of this information was held back for decades. Many think Prescott failed at his coup but his family has succeeded in turning America into a corporate, fascist government pushing democracy into the ditch. It was the plan.

Without knowing this information before writing this book I honestly had worries Reagan was attempting the same type coup when his Presidency ran wildly amuck. FDR found out about the plan and agreed to make nice with many trials for treason in the balance. Republicans allowed the New Deal to go into effect without resistance in exchange for no trials. Treasonous acts had abounded as they did from 2001 to January 2009.

Marine Corp Major General Smedley Butler, a big WWI hero, had been approached several times in 1933 by some members of ALL who added a little bit more information each time they met. Butler listened and played along, then spilled the information to the House Committee on un-American Activities, which refused to investigate or even film his testimony. I believe the sound was taped. Some American executives had been instrumental in helping set up a fascist state in Germany and Italy. Free round trips on the Hamburg-Amerikanische Paketfahrt Actien-Gesellschaft ship were offered to Americans willing to spread the corporate word over there. In addition, many such American executives gave financially to aid in those changes to fascism over there in Europe.

Prescott's banks arranged to ship gold, fuel, steel, coal and U. S. Treasury Bonds to Hitler to feed and finance his war machine. Interestingly, Prescott's investment company was called Brown Brother Harriman, and Nazi soldiers were called "Brown Shirts." I don't know if there were a connection.

Harriman, a close friend of Prescott's and a Democrat, whose brother was a NYS governor, was also part of that company which profited in grand style. The Jewish Advocate indicated the theme "war can be very profitable" which may have resonated in the mind of Prescott's grandson, George W. Bush, for Bush started two expensive, long wars with the help of numerous Jewish Americans. Even some Republicans calculated those wars would end up costing $4 trillion or more. Bush fired one of his own because the advisor said it would cost far more than $50 billion. $4 trillion is 80 times $50 billion.

In 1942, Bush and Thyssens's bank were suspected of holding gold for Nazi leaders. That bank was seized in October 1942 under Trading with the

Enemy Act. Prescott Bush continued as a director and shareholder with Thyssen, even after the U. S. joined in WWII.

Thyssen owned large German companies which profited even more by using prisoners from Auschwitz and other concentration camps as slave laborers. At least two of Prescott Bush's U. S. companies were seized by the U. S. government because "of considerable assistance to the (German) country's war effort." Back then the word "treason" was used as it should have been then and now.

Wasn't Prescott's son, George Herbert Walker Bush, serving as a U. S. pilot at the same time? Is there such a thing as a greed gene?

From 1947 through 1950, Prescott was the Connecticut Republican Finance Chairman. His jobs always seemed to have connections to ready cash as a treasurer or in this case political donations which can hide like a mole in a pile of leaves.

In 1950 Prescott ran for the U. S. Senate seat from Connecticut. He lost. In 1952, a Connecticut Republican Senator died. Republicans backed Bush as the replacement. I believe he served the balance of that term plus one more term as a U. S. Senator. With his 'high moral ground' he lashed out at Nelson Rockefeller for divorcing his first wife in 1964 to marry a much younger woman with whom he had been having an affair while still married to wife #1.

Rich, corporate individuals loved what Prescott started, the takeover of our government through various means including taking money from wars where lots of spending is secret. More than $100 billion is now missing from W's war in Iraq. Every effort by Democrats to find and capture it has been blocked by Republicans. The pattern is consistently present.

Jeb Bush

Miguel Recarey was known to most people in Florida as a Mafia figure. He set up the largest HMO in America but wanted to be bigger. A regulation kept such a company from doing more than 50% of its business with Medicare. Asked for help, Jeb Bush arranged for that regulation to be waived. The HMO quickly grew.

Patient's bills were not paid. Miguel disappeared along with hundreds of millions intended to pay Medicare bills. Additionally, $100 million in Medicare fraud was discovered. The result...more money stolen from Medicare with no punishment or recovery!

February 1, 1985... Broward Federal Savings loaned $4,565,000 to developer, J. Edward Houston, on his signature alone. On the same day the entire loan proceeds were loaned by Houston to Jeb Bush and real estate developer, Armondo Codina. A 5 story financial district building was purchased with a contract stipulating "payments would have to be made if income was sufficient." No payments were ever made. All parties were sued. Bush and Codina had to pay a total of $500,000; and they kept the building.

As a result of such loans the Broward Federal Savings thrift failed, costing taxpayers $285 million. The whole savings and loan thrift deal cost us $500 billion. For comparison: when Johnson was President our entire annual national budget was $99 billion, if my memory is correct. The thrift crimes cost more than our national budget for 2 years. Reagan and Bush, Sr. were very quiet regarding the Thrift Banks, and definitely sought no actions. Banks are almost all owned by Republicans who repeat over and over regulation is choking them. Where were regulations and enforcement when $500 billion in scamming put 130 savings and loans out of business? That money didn't evaporate. It went into the pockets of bank directors, their family members and their businesses. In most cases NO payments were made - on purpose. This goes with my expression, "Where there is a pile of money, the greedy will figure out how to take it." This failure alone added to our nation's debt immensely. Another incident showed Jeb receiving a $75,000 fee for finding a piece of real estate. He didn't find a property but received the $75,000.

Why? Why does there seem to be a pattern in the Bush family of being paid large chunks of money for basically doing nothing? Yet Florida residents voted for Jeb. Neil is not in jail. Nor is Marvin or George W. or Jeb.

There are two well recommended movies which help understand all the actions, including failure of the 130 thrifts, which along with other Republican moves, have taken our country into the Republican Great Recession. Every time Democrats try to get the economy on course and the nation moving in the correct direction in which all members of our country are doing well, our efforts are undone as the rich have their way.

"Inside Job," a Stephen Pizzo film, includes the failure of the thrifts. "Untold Story" is another similar movie by Pete Brewton. I have not seen either yet but have heard rave reviews.

Researching this type of organized theft along with internalizing the real attempt to take America into a Nazi type fascist state has been hard for me. One of the hardest parts is to see millions of Americans clamoring to support the very persons, and the party members, who are doing this to us.
Over time my mind digests what their actions have done and can do to the country I love. If you have read this far I hope you do your part to ask others to get informed. I know you have jobs and a family, and really don't want to dwell on the negative. I ask you to at least spend a few minutes a week becoming informed, and that you use your precious votes to take us away from such actions which are anything but Christian. If you think America could never become a dictatorship, you are fooling yourself.

Those who are of the mind to do such a thing will kill thousands quickly to get the herd under control. Look at how it works in Northern Africa and in the Middle East. You expect others to be compassionate and honest and to act like humans. They will not!

I purposefully have written this to be a fast read, more like conversation than a text book. My hope is to keep our country from falling deeper into a corporate, fascist web on Election day this November. We need a serious addition of Democrats to both houses of Congress and also need to maintain our leadership at the White House. Perhaps you can loan your book to others, or maybe buy a copy for them.

George Herbert Walker Bush

The 41st President of the U. S. told regulators to back off including any investigations into thrift bank losses. In 1989,to enhance backing off, President H. W. Bush dismantled "strike forces" which were good at investigating. He moved them into the Justice Department where he might have a little more influence. George, Sr. demonstrated laxity toward the perpetrators since several were close to him, or political friends.

According to articles I've read, he put his son, Marvin, in charge of spending funds for medical supplies for needy countries. The money disappeared as medical people in those countries opened packages of used needles, catheters and other used medical waste. Most Presidents would have been embarrassed.

According to articles read online, George, Sr. has been friends and business partners with the dictator kings of Saudi Arabia, King Faud bin Abdul Aziz (1982-2005,) and King Abdullah bin Abdulaziz al-Saud (2005 to Present.) Together the Kings and Bush family have been major stockholders in the Carlysle Group. I understand the Bush family was trying to arrange the sale of Allison Transmissions, a U. S. company, to the Group. Allison makes the automatic transmissions which are in most school buses, trucks, military equipment and other equipment in general. Imagine having those factories moved to the Middle East. During a possible war what would we use if Allison said, "No!" to us when we needed transmissions for military trucks to move troops, fuels, foods and supplies? Would that fit under "dumb move" in a dictionary? Why aren't America's needs considered?

I have also heard Citibank is another company with the king of Saudi Arabia as a major stockholder. That is the same king whose wife wrote the checks to pay for the lodging, foods, travel, flying lessons, etc. -all the needs of the 20 or 22 persons who were part of the 9-11 attacks on the U. S. Twin Towers and Pentagon on September 11, 2001. Our government has the specific evidence including pictures of the checks.

It was mind blowing to see President George W. Bush allow one airplane into the air with the bin Laden family aboard after the 9-11 attacks, and without questioning any of them. Why would anyone do such a thing? The bin Laden family is a rich, prominent family in Saudi Arabia, and was being protected. At least 18 of the 9-11 attackers were from Saudi Arabia. An additional item: Citibank was among the foreign banks Bush bailed out with TARP monies which had been sent in to our treasury by you and me. Would the word, "ironic" fit into the equation in which the people who paid through the nose for petroleum from a dictator ending up bailing him out? If I were President you could bet money knowing I wouldn't loan taxpayer monies to any dictator as a personal loan. And why does a multiple billionaire need any loans?

When the Amir (dictator) of Kuwait Sheikh Sabah Al-Ahmad Al-Jaber Al Sabah, a member of the same Saudi Arabian family, was about to be invaded by Iraq's Hussein, the U. S. was asked to help. According to my memory CNN news reported an oil contract equaling $18 million a year was given to George W. Bush before George, Sr. said, "Yes." to sending in our troops at our expense. CNN usually repeats news several times. I heard it only once. Did someone pull it for political reasons? The thread of getting large amounts of money in questionable ways is constant. Why wasn't the U. S. repaid for our expenses in saving Kuwait as was announced originally? The Amir is also a billionaire.

Neil Bush

In 1990 a $200 million lawsuit was brought against Neil Bush and other Silverado Banking officers for "gross negligence" in banking in bringing a $1 billion bank collapse. "Our conclusion is that Silverado was the victim of sophisticated schemes and abuses by insiders and of gross negligence by its directors and outside professionals," stated FDIC Senior Deputy General Council Douglas Jones. Neil Bush, a paid director, was ripped for "multiple conflicts of interest in approving a $132 million loan" to two business partners, then receiving a total of $650,000 in payments from them.

Walters and Good ended up taking $330 million from Silverado Banking after one bank director instructed customers how to put money into family trusts to avoid repayment to the bank. To add salt to the abuse, a top regulator cut them slack by not shutting the bank down in 1988 until after George H. W. Bush's Presidential campaign was completed. A probe was asked for but not done. What a surprise!

In a $200 million settlement Neil ended up paying only $50,000. A friend of Neil's father provided Neil with $250,000 in legal services through a legal defense fund. The attorney, Thomas Ashley, was a lobbyist for bank deregulation. How could more regulation not be needed?

Jonathan Bush

Jonathan Bush, an experienced stock broker in Massachusetts, had been ordered to stop trading because of violating state law for not registering with the state. He was "cavalier" and could not explain his failure to register. There was an arrogant attitude set forth. No punishments, fines or restrictions were noted.

Martha Stewart, a Democrat, was imprisoned when she didn't follow the rules. Why are crimes by Republicans just glossed over and ignored? Insider trading was mentioned again today in the news. Will money buy favored justice for these individuals who feed trading information back and forth illegally as they make big profits in any market setting?

Prescott Bush

In 1989 Prescott Bush was arranging for Japanese organized crime members to buy American land and businesses. Prescott received a $500,000 fee about the same time President George H. W. Bush signed a national security waiver allowing two Hughes Aircraft company satellites to go to Assets Management, a company in China owned by the Japanese Mob.

George W. Bush

In 1933 when Prescott S. Bush tried to set up the coup to overthrow our democracy hoping to transform our country to a fascist dictatorship patterned after Hitler and Mussolini's, they expected to make FDR a dummy figurehead. The "Super Secretary" would be the brains and the real decider.

Pick a dumb good ol' boy with some 'I don't give a damn swagger', one who could be slapped on the back and told, "Good job!" then do whatever the dictator wants to do. They could always point the finger at the dummy. Or there could be two secretaries like Karl Rove and Dick Cheney calling the shots. The setup is there for a takeover, especially if the Supreme Court is loaded on your side; and both houses of Congress are also right wing extremist controlled.

The candidate should have good looks like Dan Quayle, Sarah Palin, Ronald Reagan or George W. Bush with the cheerleader look.

Sadly people would vote for George Clooney, even if he were dumber than three pounds of wet cardboard! I was just making a point. Clooney is actually a cool, smart guy!

By comparison, not ready for prime time, Sarah thought Africa was a country, Paul Revere warned the British, couldn't name the three major countries in North America, and made 13 quick blunders during short interviews making her the perfect fit for John McCain's Vice Presidential sidekick! McCain, a U. S. Senator, tried helping Russia set up a port on the

Mediterranean Sea near Macedonia, even though the U. S. had spent billions over the years to prevent Russia from getting such access. As Romney would say, "It's just a business deal which is how America rolls." Isn't McCain on the defense committee? Money must trump patriotism!

The multiple billionaire Russian criminal is not allowed in the U. S. even though he was buying a U. S. sport's team. McCain tried unsuccessfully to get that visa decision overturned. The story with all the names and details was in "The Nation" magazine two or three years ago. I have misplaced my copy or I'd include more of the info. I believe "The Nation" is the oldest U. S. magazine. They dig for the truth to counter the repeated untrue information from Limbaugh, Fox "news," and a host of hired mouths.

When I heard George Bush, Sr. manipulated the Texas National Guard to have George W. moved ahead of 125,000 law abiding Texan applicants, I was furious. Back then National Guard troops were never sent out of the country into war. George W. was about to be drafted. Not only did George, Sr. have his son jumped to the head of the line, he had him put into flight school, a program costing a large portion of a million dollars per student.

Training was done on a plane which would not be used in combat making deployment to Vietnam a non-issue. George W. Bush did not show up for duty for somewhere between a year and three years. Records were played with. When I served we were constantly drilled with "AWOL over 30 days is desertion. You will spend a minimum of seven years in the stockades at Fort Leavenworth, and you will start with a dishonorable discharge!"

Special treatment happens under dictatorships, not in a democracy. The Bush family members continue acting as if we we're in a fascist dictatorship; and are allowed to get away with it. Instead of being tried as criminals which would prevent them from holding office, they end up asking for your votes. Or end up with the authority to execute an average of two U. S. prisoners a week. I think a lot more thought needs to go into the selection of our leaders. It could affect you, your friends or your family.

There is a big difference between Democrats and Republicans. First I do not believe Democrat John Edwards could get a nomination for an office; and if he did I am pretty sure Democrats wouldn't vote for him. If Edwards were a Republican he not only would be nominated, he would stand a good chance of being elected. The election of Rockefeller proved that.

With an unusually poor quarterly earnings report for Harken Oil stock NOT on file at the Securities and Exchange, George W. Bush sold $828,560 worth of that stock one week before posting the report. The stock immediately plunged 60%. When asked why he filed 8 months late, the SEC did nothing when Bush told them the report must have been lost. Right!!! Again special treatment.

In 1991, Harken was linked to a $10 billion global looting spree. Despite small size and poor performance, Harken paid Bush enormously high salaries and benefits. Bush could also buy stocks at a 40% discount. In truth, he paid nothing as his company said loans were forgiven. W. Bush bought the Texas Rangers ball team for $600,000. Taxpayers again shelled out to a Bush family member, this time $135 million for a new ballpark for the Rangers. In 1998, he sold the team for $15 million.

In 2000, there were some issues regarding the votes in Florida during the Presidential election. Election results are always determined by the local state. Florida shifted into a 24 hour cycle counting the votes. W. Bush took the case to the Supreme Court which had 5 Republicans and 4 Democrats. The 5 Republicans illegally declared Bush the President "because Florida doesn't have the time to do a count" totally usurping the rights of every Florida citizen in a decision they had no right to make. Again, that is anything but democracy. That Supreme Court decision affected every U. S. citizen in a major way.

Bush put us into two wars based on false premises and staged information. His Vice President's company, Halliburton, stepped up getting unlimited billions in contracts. Our troops went without while $100 billion went missing.

Saving oil took precedent over human safety. Bush and Cheney continued with illegal torture as a main thread in Bush's Presidency. Spending went wild with much of it off the books as the U. S. economy plunged losing up to 800,000 jobs a months. Instead of creating jobs here, Bush sent major jobs to England and Italy, (Presidential helicopters,) IRS jobs to India, top secret rocket jobs to China, and other jobs to Canada. He and other Republicans are not interested in creating jobs here in our country. Every effort to create or save jobs in the U. S. has been voted down in unison by Republicans. Their hatred for U. S. workers and unions falls back to workers demanding some rights and expecting a living wage.

With 100% control of all branches of government all years except two, Republicans ruled as right wing dictators. Troops killed in action were brought in secretly at night with no one allowed there at the airport. Bush didn't want pictures or stories out there about casualties from his wars which turned massive profits for many companies and friends. In the end, oil companies were able to keep their influence over the multiple billions of barrels of oil there. That meant his war efforts were successful.

During Bush's 8 years in office one news program stated $27 TRILLION in wealth moved to the top one or two percent, the very rich. The wealth was from stocks and 401-K's, homes and other properties. Millions of people are still hurting and at times are being driven to live in their cars. Bank of America was mentioned as the bank being the worst offender. Papers were not checked and were even signed by minimum wage people who signed documents illegally all day long, papers which would cause home owners to lose their homes. This is an example of fascism perfected. As a punishment Bush asked them how many billions they wanted from the $700 billion in TARP funds. They laugh because they know they can do illegal stuff and get away with it. Fascism doesn't include democratic ideas or ideals.

Millions of people lost their jobs. Millions lost their homes. Over 5000 real people died in Iraq; more in Afghanistan. I heard over 50,000 have had losses of arms, legs, eyes and other body parts - and hundreds of thousands have PTSD (Post Traumatic Stress Disorder.) Several troops commit suicide each week as they are jerked around by a VA that was ordered to play games with them by "Commander" Bush.

Business profits have increased as education and medical care has suffered. He had visible disdain for American workers and absolutely no empathy for those suffering, and all while claiming to be a Christian. Until Governor Rick Perry overtook his record, George W. Bush executed more citizens than any governor in U. S. history. The vast majority were minorities, some even children; at least one was mentally challenged.

Democrats tried and tried to get more border guards for the U. S. borders, specifically for the U. S/Mexican border. In the two years' window (2006-2008) when Democrats had majorities in the House and Senate, they wrote and passed a bill in which 7000 border guards were authorized. Expecting another W. Bush veto, it was sent to the White House. Imagine their surprise and delight when Bush signed it into law. As the guards finished training, Bush sent them to Iraq. He was having trouble getting volunteers to go fight his loony wars which with multiple back to back deployments caused many divorces. Some served 4 or 5 tours with little or no time between tours. Strict regulations governing deployment were ignored.

After 9-11, security was elevated to a higher level especially at airports. In all honesty those 9-11 terrorists were all Arabs from the Middle East. Republicans in general will do anything to keep our government from having more employees even if they are truly needed.

Not wanting more employees hired in his name, Bush said we could save money hiring a private business to provide the security at the airports to check mainly on Arab persons. Maybe when he hired a French company he didn't know France now has an estimated 7,000,000 Arab Muslims as citizens.

Terrorists can now apply to the French security firm and after being hired have total access to the airport and planes. Sweet!

Despite strong repeated pleas from Democrats, President Bush gave our top-top secret rocket contracts to China instead of an American company. It must be he heard China say it wanted to get into the lucrative missile business for customers like Iran and North Korea. I am not making this up.

The IRS employees in the U. S. cost more than workers in India would cost. With low income, the Indian workers can make a little extra when they have information like your name, address, Social Security number, bank account name, number and location, and an idea of how much money you make. Have you ever wondered how people in Russia, Northern Africa or India are able to get your information so they can drain your accounts? I hope the ones who voted for him are the ones who have their information stolen! That would be some sweet justice.

In August, just before 9-11, Counterterrorism Security Group Leader Richard Clark sent W. Bush a note saying an attack on America was imminent. He asked the President for a face to face meeting to discuss the details. He made other such attempts but was ignored every time. Then on August 6th, 2001, he sent President George W. Bush a notice with huge lettering saying a message something like: "AN ATTACK IN AMERICA IS IMMINENT AND WILL INVOLVE SOMETHING LIKE FLYING LARGE AIRCRAFT INTO BUILDINGS!" It was 11 and a half pages, much longer than the regular 2 or 3 pages.

When a stressed CIA agent read the message to Bush while Bush vacationed in Texas he was blown off with, "All right you've covered your ass, now." Bush had so far taken vacation 41% of his time as President. Now he was on back to back vacations for two weeks or so.

Simultaneously Vice President Dick Cheney spent the entire month on vacation in Wyoming. I personally wonder if they purposefully ignored the warnings so as to have a reason to go to war in the Middle East. When one thinks of The Project of the New American Century, which met in 1997, it is not that far-fetched.

During Bush's vacation 9-11 occurred. Try to imagine what you would have done if you had been the President and had received all those warnings. Bin Laden had been trained in the engineering of skyscraper buildings here in the United States. He knew how to weaken a building to collapse it. We knew that. And we know the Twin Towers located right next to Wall St. are symbolic of the American business way of life.

We knew bin Laden was hell bent to attack the United States. In 1991, an attempt was made in the basement of one of the towers to topple it. If a sixth grader were given this information, what might that student determine? I wonder if those who voted for W. Bush as President would have him be their surgeon if a college had given him "gentleman's C's" diploma allowing him to be a certified surgeon. Would you allow him to do surgery on your daughter or son?

The price of gasoline in NYS went from $1.10 to around $4.50 under Bush. The price of a barrel of oil rose from around $18 or $20 to around $108, going as high as $149 under George W. Bush. The Saudi Arab oil producers stated they could live with a price of $25 a barrel for a long, long time. Who convinced them to change their minds thereby increasing the price of the gas portion of a gallon between 2001 and 2009 by 600%?

Called the Great Recession, it is seen by me as a purposeful means every 30 to 50 years to shift wealth to the rich. Wall St. and banks overextended bringing about another $700 billion in corporate welfare spending to keep them from failing. We are likely as close to a fascist government as we ever have been with workers wages (purchasing power) at 1980 levels, a 32 year regression. It puts employees in their place, weakens unions and makes people beg for jobs.

Corporations want capitalism when they are doing well; corporate welfare and corporate socialism when they are failing.

A quick $700 billion for crooks at banks, investment corporations and insurance companies - - sure.....but not even 100 or 50 billion to fix our infrastructure which would quickly create needed jobs and boost the economy. It would certainly increase our safety, too, and save money in the long run. Republicans are doing this to us on purpose.

The GOP opposed the Democratic bill for less than $3 billion which saved the U. S. auto business and gave jobs to millions. I believe no Republicans spoke against the $700 billion bailout to the crooks who caused our economic downturn in banks and on Wall St. They all voted in unison against funding infrastructure bills per the Grover Norquist pledge they had all signed with one or two exceptions. The pledge to Norquist means more to them than our Constitution.

The President, who says we don't need more money for education because "The children is learning!" hasn't a clue about much of anything. He was a right wing's perfect Presidential candidate.

John Boehner

Speaker of the House John Boehner is 2nd in line to be President of the United States. Why would his fellow GOP representatives vote to make him Speaker when it is obvious he is either depressed, or has some other condition which causes him to break out in tears time after time? That condition should present itself well when he sits down for tough negotiations with world leaders.

A person that close to possibly becoming President should have respect for the Presidency, yet in September 2011, Boehner, for the first time in our country's history, refused President Obama's official request to address Congress. He did not even respond. Boehner also declined what would be a normal trip on Air Force One, the President's aircraft.

The news media noted these actions as outward expressions of "I have no intention of working with or physically being near you." Some expressed opinions which included the actions as bringing a racial tone emanating from a wider circle of the GOP.

Regardless of whether or not any new bill regarding elected Congressmen and Senators doing insider stock trading, an official judgment was given stating those same elected people are already denied insider trading by the original law(s.) Speaker of the House Boehner has been reported to have made at least 5 investments in companies which are the likely bidders on building the Keystone Pipeline, the same ones lobbying for its approval. One investment is $50,000 or more. The sense is Boehner, as Speaker, had lots of insider information not publicly out there.

While accusing President Obama of not bringing the economy back fast enough, an economy destroyed by many of the same group of Republicans, Boehner has been the impediment, the very person holding up any job creation bills from even being brought up for vote in the House. It's like disabling all the fire trucks, then blaming the fireman for not putting out fires quickly enough.

Charles Koch
David Koch

Bill Gates (Microsoft and Gateway) is the richest American. Warren Buffet, an announced Democrat, is number 2. Warren developed Berkshire Hathaway into a company which is like a wide ranging mutual fund. He and Bill have together formed a foundation used to help less fortunate persons on Earth, especially in Africa. They have each pledged billions to it.

Third and fourth most wealthy Americans are Charles and David Koch (say Coke) with $50 billion and growing fast. They continue to acquire wealth from each of us through extremely lucrative hedge funds which make fortunes from imaginary dollars used in manipulating markets, particularly in oil products. Hedge funds hold special privileges, tax wise, privileges which Republicans will not allow to be changed.

Taxes on such "earnings" are non-existent or extremely low. I'm not even sure they need the "Bush tax cuts" to avoid paying taxes.
David and Charles likely are the most influential persons having input into U. S. elections, now even more so with the 5 to 4 Citizens United case which allows any entity, including corporations or even countries, to contribute as much money as they wish to sway any U. S. election. If North Korea and Iran could pony up enough money, they could buy our elections. Or Germany and Italy could join with the wealthy right wing persons to convince everyone fascism is a good thing. They are very cleaver with ads, and could get a candidate like Romney elected to make the transition from a democracy happen. All they need is ignorant voters to do it the official way.

Among the numerous cleverly named foundations they own and control are: The Heritage Foundation, The Cato Institute, American Crossroads run by Karl Rove, The Tea Party, started and managed for them by former Republican House Majority Leader, Dick Armey from Texas, and Crossroads GPS, another also run by Karl Rove.

What most Americans really don't understand is just how few Republicans control the party. The so-called 1% of taxpayers is only around 320,000 or some such low number. The amounts of monies they make are beyond enormous, so they do pay a proportionately higher amount in taxes – and they should..well, at least when they did pay taxes. After all, taxes are based on the amount of income. They use government infrastructures and services the most. Think of airports as a for instance. Airports are expensive to build, maintain and staff.

How many airline tickets do minimum wage workers buy? Why shouldn't the rich who use airports very often pay the most? The rich have the resources to hire professionals who know how to control the herd. The plan is delivered by someone like Grover Norquist, a person there to whip everyone into compliance. Those who don't conform are eliminated narrowing the party line.

Mouth pieces like Ann Coulter, Druggie Limbaugh, Ari Fleischer and others are fed the line to say, and they go out and deliver. Have you noticed how within two hours they are all spouting the exact same words?

Thank yous can be delivered in various ways. A wealthy person supporting the author's story may buy a large number of such a person's books, some of which can exceed $100 in price. Buying a few high priced books is a legal way to say thank you easily. Or an author can be given a gift, or hired to do a job without expectations. I have no such arrangements, but invite them!

Unless an author is well known, he or she likely will never take in enough royalties to pay for time or expenses involved in a book's creation. If somewhat successful, a year's work could gross $3000 to 5000. I expected it would be several times that.

By the way Democrats have authors, some with talk shows, and some representatives who also give our side of current issues; but I believe only a fraction of the money is involved when compared with Republican counterparts.

I would understand people saying I have a Democratic slant – and that without doubt is true. But what I do and see others do, who represent the Democratic side, is deal with truth. I do not see that on the Republican side.

As shown by my first registering as a Conservative, and by looking into the Tea Party when it came out, I can say I've had an opened mind when it comes to parties. The differences are just too stark and unacceptable.

I do take notice and respect Republicans who admit President George W. Bush and Republicans trashed America with uncontrolled spending for years. But then they immediately expect you to turn the page and think everything from January 2009 is on President Obama. They ignore the ongoing costs of two expensive wars, and the one TRILLION dollars a year cost just to cover interest attributed to Bush's elective wars.

And that figure is growing. Bills established previously have to be paid regardless who is President. Joblessness set up by Bush brings its own set of costs as has always been the case throughout history. A dead or floundering economy needs to be stimulated. A brand new car with a flat tire needs a little attention.

Almost everyone knows there are hot button issues which can easily set people off. Stir up voters with religious beliefs, or threaten them with higher taxes. I could go on about making a case some don't volunteer much in our military; or some export our jobs and manufacturing companies, and our limited natural resources. Those very persons wave our flag inferring Democrats aren't patriotic. Based on what?

Most military volunteers are poor, working people who do not want our jobs, factories or resources exported. Wouldn't you think voters could see through such baloney?

My economics' courses showed equipment and auto dealers make profits from 25% to 35%. On an $80,000 tractor, a dealer can profit $20,000 or more. Milk prices continue to rise putting more profits into the corporate coffers while farmers exist until they fail.

Let's say the farm equipment dealer makes millions in profits a year – and because of unbelievably high Bush tax cuts, avoided paying any fair share in taxes for twelve years. As a businessman, who wants the tax cuts permanently written into law, he leads the farmers through the Tea Party to help assure he keeps those tax breaks.

Farmers are good hard working people who for many decades have voted Republican. For a day off, o. k., a part of a day, they go to the Tea Party gathering for a hot dog and soda and to socialize... and some brain washing. Many of the farmers end up supporting those who make huge profits from them. Don't be bought for the price of a hotdog and a soda. You should be getting a higher price for your milk, and a big discount on machinery would help you help America. A dealer can spend only so many millions in profits while you flounder. Profits on milk go almost exclusively to large corporate owners, not to farmers who have done the investing and the hard work.

I worked from age 8 to 18 on dairy farms and know the routine. Farmers deserve respect and our thanks. I wish they realized how much Democrats have moved to the right in the past 4 decades, away from the often unfair "liberal" label. I personally don't know a single liberal. Democrats also respect your work, something Republican higher ups lack. You are nothing but the slaves who deliver profits to them! Prices they pay you prove that.

Republicans are now so far to the right they are into the fascist, Nazi region. I am guessing you are so busy surviving you don't really see the full picture and how you are being used.

Republican advertising is cleverly done. I am financially conservative but had no idea of the real history of the Republicans and Conservatives. I admit at a young age, I was drawn in to that "responsible image" they set forth in words. Boy, after studying and reading did I realize what a farce they are. They are great story tellers if fiction is your thing.

Republicans, in their minds, are the smart persons who know when it is o. k. to ignore laws set up for controlling other people. Business should rule without regulation, and workers should know their place and not make waves.

Because of all the "good they've done" Republicans are entitled to live high. Democrats do not oppose business, or making profits. We do feel any business without guiding parameters will continue to push the limits. Not everyone, but way too many. Democrats also go with our Constitution which expressly says "of the People, by the People and for the People," not "of, by and for the Corporations" which is the Fascist model. We like and believe in democracy, not in a **"Citizens United"** corporate stance inconsistent with the Constitution.

Below is a May 30, 2012 "IN OUR OPINION" editorial reprinted courtesy of **The Daily Star**, Oneonta, N. Y. entitled "Citizens United should be overturned."

Twenty-two states - led by New York - and the District of Columbia are pushing for the Supreme Court to reconsider its 2010 Citizens United decision.

The 2010 ruling struck down much of the 2002 campaign-finance reform law, essentially lifting a federal ban on corporate campaign spending. It allowed each corporation to claim its "personhood" and the right to spend untold sums as part of First Amendment guarantees.

We have seen the results of the court's decision. It has turned our federal election system into a free-for-all for nameless, faceless corporate spending and the eruption of super political action committees disguised as independent entities.

And this is not just a Republican spending frenzy, as some may think, though a majority of the money spent by these super PACs has gone to the causes of GOP candidates.

According to a story by The Associated Press, in May alone pro-President Barack Obama PAC Priorities USA Action--run by former Obama White House aides--spent $2.4 million on advertisements condemning GOP presidential candidate Mitt Romney. The group had received $10 million by the end of March, the AP story said.

For the Romney camp, $4.3 million was spent for ads in May by Restore Our Future--run by former Romney advisers. It has amassed at least $51 million since its creation.

These figures show the blatant disregard by corporations for the ability of independent voters to act and contribute for themselves as American citizens.

It does not seem enough for these super PACS and corporations that the candidates raise millions in more-conventional campaigning, such as fundraisers and donations from actual free-thinking people who want a stake in their future.

It is good to see states take up the fight against the Supreme Court's ruling. While they are hinging their arguments on keeping state campaign spending laws intact--specifically in a Montana state court ruling on corporate expenditures--the states' concerns offer the court an opportunity to reconsider its federal decision.

In the high court's defense, the justices have indicated they will consider whether the Montana ruling against state corporate campaign spending conflicts directly with the Citizens United decision or if state spending should be deemed separate from federal campaign contribution law. And if that means a re-examination and clarification of their decision, the justices are moving in the right direction.

Peter Schurman, spokesman for a group called Free Speech For People, correctly summed up the need for action in an AP story: "There is a growing bipartisan consensus that Citizens United needs to be overturned, and Montana is leading the way. The Supreme Court has an opportunity to revisit Citizens United here. That is important because there is evidence everywhere that unlimited spending in our elections creates both corruption and the appearance for corruption.

—

The wealthy 320,000 have control of most radio, t. v., newspaper and magazine companies. Do you remember Michael Moore had arranged t. v. time to play one of his movies days before an election? At the last second, the company owned by a Republican, canceled the contract thereby controlling the voters' right to hear and see a balanced presentation about the candidate.

Voters are given sound bites which are hoped to persuade a vote in one direction. You are considered to be dumb enough to be convinced. It is a known fact people have a tendency to believe a story if it is repeated over and over to them. Republicans repeat known lies for years.

One example is, "Democrats are weak on national defense." That is such a lie. I don't believe either side is weak. Who got bin Laden? Who got the most terrorists? Who replaced Bush's worn out military equipment? Not Bush! Yes, replacing equipment worn out by sand and heat added to our national debt a couple trillion; and don't forget a trillion a year for interest on Bush's debts times three years so far. Maybe someone should blame Bush for letting us get into such a weak state of readiness; yet the GOP yammers on about Obama's spending. Someone has to stand up and be responsible. You don't have to be one of the persons blaming the wrong person.

Fifty years ago Republicans represented about 85% of registered voters. There is a reason they are now only 31.25 percent of registered voters. More and more voters are finding out only a handful (my rough guess is less than 1000) make the decisions which all other party members are then to internalize and support. I, for one, don't like to be told what and how to think. I also believe good ideas come from everywhere. Those self-appointed "smart" people make one dumb decision after another. We lose lives and treasure.

Each party has to have a set of beliefs which are the main pillars governing all decisions; then those beliefs should be stood behind, every time. The only exceptions are when an evolution of thought makes a newer position the logical choice. I don't mean just for winning one election or any other such a temporary change. People like and deserve steady thinking.

I see elections in which candidates take a different position so the end justifies the means. Lies and deceit become the norm. Flip-flopping because of the way the wind is blowing creates weakness. The lady legislator from Maryland, a Republican, said it best: "Mitt hasn't changed his mind since the last time!"

The ideas within the GOP now come from a universal greed theme with entitlement for the rich. Those ideas drift toward the support of corporations, and with strong feelings against working people who are basically viewed as unappreciative slaves who don't behave. All ideas stem from those thoughts.

Billionaires Charles and David Koch have a vicious dislike for those who toil in our factories, or those who dry clean their clothing, or serve their meals. A year ago the brothers dumped many millions of dollars into matters in Ohio and Wisconsin. Contracts negotiated for decades were illegally overturned by Republican majorities as Democrats put up a strong fight. When voters don't get out and vote, that is what happens.

Every Republican votes – every time. The GOP wins elections at least half the time just by showing up. There are usually dollars in the balance for them in the end.

Governor John Kasich, of Ohio, and Governor Scott Walker, of Wisconsin, may end up being voted out of office through a proposition election. The workers in the states finally got mad. One state has had its workers' rights restored. Had they got out and voted in the first place, they wouldn't have had to put up the fight and in a weakened position. Staying strong is easier than making a comeback after being weak.

Two billionaires have been the ones with the most pull in the entire Republican Party. The concept of rule by one family was a main theme opposed in the formation of the government in the new country, America. As we can easily see, wealth has powerful influence. Will we let America be bought; or is democracy still a good idea?

Democrats discuss our ideas, sometimes loudly. Some see that as weakness; I see it as a strategy to come up with the best ideas most of us can support.

A perfect year for me would be for every worker asked to provide a product, or a service to every person like Charles and David Koch, to tell them, "No! Go grow or make your own!" They would very quickly learn to have and show respect to those who toil to make their lives easy. They'd have no time to trade stocks, and even if they did, their money wouldn't buy them anything.

I know this is not really likely but we could work toward that end. Workers should buy and control the companies where they work. That would be a good start.

An added 6-9-12 comment: With $40,000,000 in big money donations from the Koch brothers and other fat cats, Scott Walker was able to keep his governorship in a voter forced recall election earlier this week. His Democratic opponent spent $3,000,000. Was the election bought?

With the Supreme Court "five" Republicans allowing unlimited secret spending by any person, country or business in their Citizens United decision, the United States as a democracy appears to be in the most jeopardy ever. Workers too busy to become informed, or to vote, can expect to see a fascist takeover of America. This has been the end goal of Republicans as they drift quickly more and more to the right. And pretty much everyone knows elections can be bought in most cases.

This is not just a scare tactic on my part. Preventing a fascist takeover of the country I love and served is the reason I am writing this book. If you care, you need to vote to save America - and get others to vote, too. Was it Benjamin Franklin who said something like, "We have a democracy as long as the people stand up and want to keep it.?"

Greed is a factor which drives some persons beyond patriotism or any caring for other individuals. The need to kill, torture or imprison others is just a matter of course in acquiring enormous wealth and control of the herd. Look around the world to see dozens of examples. Hopefully we are not as close as I am seeing it.

Rupert Murdock

The owner of the previously mentioned Clearwater and Fox News also owns The New York Post, The Wall Street Journal and the now defunct and embarrassed London World News; and many, many other radio and t. v. stations along with more print media. The World News was closed down after it was found they were hacking into computers of celebrities and into government computers, too. Both he and his son, who was in charge at the London paper, denied knowing anything about it. That seems to be the standard answer a wealthy man gives when such a scandal pops up.

His stations have not played Dixie Chicks' music since Natalie responded to answer an audience question at a concert in England saying she was embarrassed by President Bush's actions. I immediately went out and bought their CD without knowing what was on it. It is excellent! Support of those who speak up is very important, and one of our important rights.

Businesses and persons who are sold radio or t. v. rights to our airways are required to provide equal access for political purposes. During the 2008 election season with a Republican President and a Republican FCC Commissioner, it was treated as a normal fascist event when Rupert pulled the Michael Moore movie I referenced earlier. "Laws, rules and regulations are for the other people," is an unwritten GOP motto. Is this the arrogance you want to represent you and your country?

Sarah Palin

Presidential candidate John McCain was desperate for a kick in his ratings so, having seen the interest Democrats had shown in candidate Hillary Clinton, he looked around for a queen to have as his Vice President. In Alaska, there was a beauty queen who was elected as governor in a state with about the population of Syracuse, N. Y. With its income from the sale of oil from property owned by U. S. citizens, there was enough money flowing to cover all costs of government, and to send out checks with five figures each to each citizen twice a year. She boasted she had a balanced budget. Duh! Comments on television indicated she often didn't go to the office but stayed home in pajamas.

Sarah was very critical of government pork and waste, yet saw a very expensive 4 lane thruway built to the location where the "Bridge to Nowhere" was to be built. Nobody uses the thruway, yet I heard it is staffed

24/7/365. U. S. taxpayers should be told thank you for all the bacon we provided for a totally useless project.

The $320,000,000 "bridge to nowhere" was to go from the end of the thruway to the island, Gravina, with 50 inhabitants, people who didn't want it. They owned boats and aircraft to cross the very short distance from island to mainland; and when it was cold (this IS Alaska) they simply drove across the ice. There also was a ferry every 15 to 30 minutes. Republicans in Congress did approve the funding which Alaskans were too embarrassed to take.

Just like you, I am convinced Sarah is against wasteful government pork! Right! As one politician said, "A billion here, a billion there and pretty soon you're talking real money!" With so many phonies out there it is easy for "Saturday Night Live" to find material each week.

Rick Perry

9/12/11 CNN Re: previous Presidential debate...According to Rick Perry Social Security is a Ponzi scheme. There is no question he would abolish it if he gets the chance. Count that as a truth for the upper level Republicans. Just before elections they are suddenly for Social Security and Medicare, and can be heard saying, "We MUST save Social Security and Medicare!" They do it every time. Also, gasoline prices, controlled mostly by Republican investors, drop just before elections. There has been a large glut of petroleum in the past several years as the prices spiraled upward to over $4.00 again. After the election gasoline will go up again.

Rick Perry has executed more citizens as governor of Texas than any U. S. governor in our history. Governor George W. Bush had previously held the record with about 2 per week over two terms. Most were minority persons in both cases.

For many years Perry leased a large hunting camp which had a large boulder at the entrance. On the boulder was painted, "N-----head." Perry said he painted over it many years ago. Neighbors said, "a few days ago." Racism and telling lies is a common Republican thread. Such topics are discussed with arrogant smiles.

Are you as puzzled as I am when minorities campaign and vote for such candidates?

Michael Powell

Republican Secretary of State Colin Powell's son, Michael, was President George W. Bush's pick to be the FCC Commissioner. Powell didn't do anything to help American citizens in his job. Conversely, he did represent corporations well.

Willard Mitt Romney

Willard Romney was very closely tied to his religion as a Mormon. Brigham Young, a strong racist and "one who talked directly with God," was seen as a super being by Mitt and was an acknowledged hero to the 21 year old Willard who worked to spread the religion which allowed men to marry any number of women. Willard, or Mitt, even went to France for a year or so to broaden the religion's footprint.

Brigham Young was born in 1801 and died in 1877. Romney stated the mixing of a white man with a Black woman meant instant death should be expected.

In my view racists are in the bully family. Right wing Republicans, Ku Klux Klan members, Nazis and Mormons have fit the image for a long time. Hitler led eager followers who stood against minorities, those with handicapping conditions, and gays. As a regular occurrence handicapped individuals and those with low I. Q's were given lethal injections in hospitals.

Men are superior to women. How does that explain Blacks, Hispanics, women or gays being registered as Republicans? I would tend not to associate with those who drag people down roads behind pickups, beat up and terrorize women and otherwise kill, injure and humiliate the aforementioned individuals or groups; or support the very party which works tirelessly to diminish their rights, incomes, hopes and futures. Nothing like cheering for your abusers!

Mitt Romney became wealthy as sole owner of the company, Bain Capital, which ended American businesses starting in 1984, either closing them, or moving them abroad. A GOP sponsored law made it so U. S. companies, like GE, would pay NO U. S. taxes. Republicans passed a law which actually pays the companies to move out of the U. S. They give them our monies! Romney supported such legislation. Now some workers who lost their jobs because of Romney, will vote to support him. In this case most will not. They have bitter memories!

Smart, to some people is making money continuously by being the force causing those jobs to be moved out of the U. S. I don't think I could live with myself or face those who are without jobs because of what I did for a profit; then ask them for their votes.

Actual businesses still operating within the U. S. set up phony addresses in the Cayman Islands, the Netherlands, Ireland or some other places with Romney's help, specifically to avoid paying U. S. taxes. He does not want to show us how patriotic he was over the past 20 years or so by showing us his tax returns.

Romney is known as the Etch-a-Sketch candidate for changing his mind so many times. He is always for what you are for.

Republican Christine O'Donnell from Maryland got it right when she said "Romney hasn't changed his mind since the last time." If you stop to think of it, Romney, like Reagan and George W. did, changes his mind to accommodate whoever is making a suggestion. In that regard, he is the perfect candidate to be manipulated by his handlers, his advisors.

Showing he is about five decades behind the times in foreign affairs, Romney identified Russia as our greatest threat. Didn't we have enough of that thinking during the first 8 years of this century? Do voters have no pride or concern for their country?

The word, "ignorant" comes from ignore. Ignoring history, ignoring truths, ignoring wise judgment takes us there. If voters are shallow enough to vote for Romney, they will likely vote more Republicans into Congress, too, setting up a real full house.

Appointments to the Supreme Court will then possibly see Republicans go from a 5-4 advantage to a 7-2 advantage stacking the Court for decades to come. At that point there will be an optimum opportunity to finish changing our country from a democracy to the fascist dictatorship already planned back in the 1930's or earlier.

Top Republicans have long range plans which unfortunately have been well underway for more than a century. How close are they now to critical mass? I wish I were wrong!

Ronald Reagan

Ronald Reagan was always one to seek attention. In college he was purported to have posed nude in the interest of art. His resolve apparently wasn't much. He changed positions more than Tina Turner dancing in a number 5 hurricane.

He was for labor and working people when he was president of SAG, the Screen Actors' Guild. Was it for attention among those in Hollywood? With a little guidance this once Democrat gleefully fired almost every air traffic controller when they stood their ground over working conditions. They were not looking for higher pay. They wanted more persons hired to cut the overtime demanded of them in a very stressful job.

Air traffic controllers simultaneously guide thousands of airplanes into and out of airports on several runways. With more traffic than the airports were designed to handle aircraft are crossing at various heights as they are guided to a runway and a "parking spot."

Weather, security issues, late aircraft and mechanical issues are but a few of matters which must be contended with. As a group, air traffic controllers had a very high divorce rate, alcohol use and abuse, a high suicide rate and other health issues related to stress. For years their issues were ignored, so as allowed in a democracy and in free enterprise, they drew the line and said, "No more!"

No one expected all striking controllers to be fired, but Reagan, in a macho move and ignoring real issues, made the situation worse – even more unsafe by hiring persons with no experience. His lack of caring for working people is a strong thread in Republican thinking, especially with those right wing fascists who don't like democracy, those wanting corporate control of everything.

His handlers were easily able to guide him into doing what was "right for

America." He saw himself as a John Wayne, but John Wayne got things done in logical and caring ways.

Elvis Presley was photographed writing a check for millions of dollars to our federal treasury. His rate was 91% on the upper end. He made a positive comment about his country saying (paraphrased) "This is America, and well worth it!" He didn't mind paying taxes to the country he loved and served in the U. S. Army.

For years Reagan admonished people with, "Every person should pay a fair share in taxes." A reporter finally held up copies of Reagan's tax forms for several years. On income of many millions President Reagan had paid absolutely nothing! So much for his phony drivel!

President Kennedy had dropped the top tax rate from 91% to around 72%. Reagan took the top rate down to 36 or 39%. That was huge considering the rich use our infrastructure the most.

With his handlers slapping his back every time he did what they wanted, he thought maybe one of the faces on Mt. Rushmore should be converted to his likeness. Even though he was always referred to as a "B" actor that didn't stop him from thinking he was the greatest.

Communism was taking its toll on Russia and its satellite countries. As they collapsed Reagan's handlers tried to say Reagan caused their collapse. That's about like taking credit for rain after doing a rain dance. It was going to happen anyway!

A President is not supposed to carry on military actions secretly without the approval of Congress. Reagan continuously lied to Americans even arrogantly adding with a smirk, "There ain't no smoking gun!" to his denials. He lied to us about national defense. Why didn't that anger the same people who got very upset when Bill Clinton lied about a personal matter, not about our national defense? Why wasn't Reagan impeached and tried for treason? The Iran-Contra deal wasn't the end of such dealings. Reagan illegally accepted an expensive California property, then quietly used millions of our tax dollars there before returning to that address. Keep in mind the expression, "Power corrupts. Absolute power absolutely corrupts!"

You or I would have spent many years in jail had we done what he had done, yet Republicans worship him as a god. I think we all know what would have happened if a Democrat did those things. Democrats, with myself included, want all criminals to be dealt with with blind justice whether Republican or Democrat.

Changing the name of The George Washington International Airport to Reagan's name by Republicans was an affront to Washington's family and the value our country puts on legal contracts like the one signed with Washington's heirs when they donated the land for the airport.

George Washington fought in the field for America – and owned the land. What war did Reagan volunteer to fight in? Or the Republicans who callously overtook the tribute to Washington? Few Republicans have served compared with Democrats. Look at the list showing who put our country into the wars in the Middle East.

Rick Santorum

Rick Santorum would be considered a nut job by most people for his out of the mainstream ideas, so how did he accumulate some votes as he did in the Republican Presidential primaries? Here's how. The U. S. has a sector of voters who think as Rick does, and they show up for every election!

He claims first to be a Christian, then turns around and lies saying government monies are being used for abortions. He knows that is not true. Rick takes a superior attitude over women as he talks as if he has the right to control them. He opposes women having the right to use ANY form of birth control. No exceptions!

He opposes Social Security, Medicare and pretty much everything normal people favor. In his last effort to get elected to the U. S. Senate from Pennsylvania, he was trounced by Pennsylvania's voters.

If Rick Santorum had been able to secure the Republican Presidential nomination, right wingers would have spent a billion or more to get him elected. Isn't it ironic for one who says the government should stay out of our lives to be telling us exactly how we should be living when it comes to personal choices?

Do you consider a person telling you you can't do something like chose to use birth control, an act of a bully? Do you want our government to drift toward Santorum's beliefs – or are you smart enough to make your own choices?

Below is a February 17, 2012 "In Our Opinion" editorial reprinted courtesy of **The Daily Star**, Oneonta, N. Y. entitled "Santorum's world scary for women."

In presidential candidate Rick Santorum's ideal world:

There would be no use of contraception. Not for young people, not for married people putting off having a child for financial reasons, not for women who benefit medically by taking the pill...nobody.

No women would be allowed in combat situations in the military, but they're capable of "flying small planes."

Women achieving success outside of the traditional homemaker role would be considered having fallen prey to a "radical feminist" doctrine.

In Santorum's bizarre world, "father knows best" isn't an old TV show, but rather a new idea of what America should be.

Gee, we wonder why Santorum, in his disastrous re-election campaign for the Senate in 2006, garnered only 39 percent of female votes while losing by 18 points overall.

In a 2006 televised interviewed, Santorum said he has voted for contraception, "although I don't think it works. ...I think it's harmful to our society to have a society that says that sex outside of marriage is something that should be encouraged or tolerated."

Tolerated?

Tolerated by whom? Who's to decide whether it's OK to have pre-marital sex or post-marital sex or non-marital sex. Mr. Santorum? You?

He has defined contraception as "a license to do things in a sexual realm that is counter to how things are supposed to be."

Oh really? Who decides how things "are supposed to be?"

Apparently in Santorum's ideal world, disadvantaged women should not aspire to get an education.

"The notion that college education is a cost-effective way to help poor, low-skill, unmarried mothers with high school diplomas or GEDs move up the economic ladder is just wrong," he said.

The only criterion in the workplace should be whether a woman can do a job, not whether she has a paucity of testosterone.

Santorum frets that men in combat situations would not be able to function at top efficiency because their chivalrous nature would make them overly protective of their female compatriots.

"I do have concerns about women in frontline combat," he said. "I think that can be a very compromising situation, where people naturally may do things that may not be in the interests of the mission because of other types of emotions that are involved."

Virginia Gov. Bob McDonnell - albeit a Mitt Romney supporter - said his daughter in the service has faced combat situations and is doing just fine, thank you.

"She did a great job, was in some risky situations," McDonnell said, "and yet endured and led, and I'm proud of her."

Rick Santorum's ideal world doesn't make us proud, it just makes us scared.

—

Richard M. Nixon

Richard Nixon, to me, was a very cold, pompous, I can do whatever I want President. Faced with impeachment for planning and carrying out a break-in into the Democratic Headquarters, he resigned a disgraced President who had broken all kinds of laws. Again, a Republican felon received no jail time, fines or penalties.

If one listens to some of Nixon's comments it is obvious he did not care for Jewish people. He said so knowing he was being recorded.

Like most Republicans he looked at women as inferior. He once asked why we waste money educating women. I mention things like this so you can have a sense of how Republicans and Conservatives have thought throughout the years.

A couple months ago a Congressional committee of all white men refused, even under pressure, to let even one woman testify before them. The committee was to discuss women's issues.

Muslims have similar feelings about women and their rights. Women can't drive, be educated, go out without permission, must walk behind men, are required to cover up with a burka, and on and on. Some Arab women have been given some rights in more recent years. Republicans tried to put off giving women the right to vote by offering to let Black *men vote instead. Apparently, Republicans thought of women at a level below Black men in the early 1900's.*

An ironic note: Nixon complained about proposed cancer research funding saying, "I'll sign it if you get it down to a reasonable level!" I believe the $3 million annual amount was dropped to $1 million. His wife, Pat, died of cancer.

Chapter 8   <u>MEET SOME DEMOCRATS</u>

Franklin Delano Roosevelt

President Obama was second to FDR in inheriting a mess to clean up. In each case Republicans had allowed the economy to collapse after a continued unsustainable super-favorable climate for corporations. Several right wing Republicans had liked what Italy and some other European countries were attempting with fascism. After WWII ended conditions in Italy and elsewhere worsened with terrible inflation, unemployment and poverty. Sounds a lot like what happened here during the first eight years of this century, doesn't it?

Mussolini grabbed power as dictator for 20 years. No elections were allowed. He organized the Fascist Party often referred to as a corporate state.

Each of 13 corporations was represented in the government. Private properties were taken when the Blackshirts, or the minister of corporations, Benito Mussolini, decided.

The government was of, by and for corporations, the anti-Communist, anti-Socialist party. Opponents were tortured, sent to camps or killed. Strikers were disciplined as Mussolini prepared to build a new Roman Empire with Hitler's help.

At the end of WWII Italians hanged him leaving him there for all to see. As most dictators do, he left Italy a defeated, destroyed country.

As I write this there are American right wingers who want to emulate Mussolini's path. Even Jim Cramer on CNBC, the stock channel, refers to our government often as a "government of, by and for the corporations." The driving force is GREED. Along with greed the sense of power over others is a factor to satisfy their egos.

Against great odds FDR worked to put America back on course from the Great Depression as Republicans tried to undermine his efforts. Retired people had been unable to save for retirement because of low pay. Over the centuries 151 other countries had faced the same circumstances – and in the end set up a social security system forcing workers to save for their own retirements instead of looking elsewhere for financial help.

Our program is a nearly perfect program. Income has to be adjusted occasionally by modifying the cap, age of eligibility and the percentage deducted. It costs around one-half of 1% to administer compared with 40 to 60% by insurance companies.

The CCC (Civilian Conservation Corp) provided productive work to the unemployed. Parks we use today were constructed, like our area Gilbert Lake State Park in Laurens, New York. Thousands of acres of trees were planted. We continue to benefit from that work. Manufacturing for WWII helped the economy pick up from the doldrums it had been stuck in.

Today President Obama faces majorities in the House, the Senate because of the need for 60 votes, and the Supreme Court which fights every effort he makes to coax the economy to expand.

On the very first day in session after President Obama's election, the Republican leaders of the House and Senate pledged to making the re-election of President Obama an impossibility their number one issue above everything else. They have stuck to that effort in complete unison. Republicans will not vote for anything which will help the country or add jobs. They will trash the U. S. thinking people are dumb enough to believe them as they 100% blame Obama.

John Fitzgerald Kennedy

President JFK was likely the most loved President ever both in the U. S. and worldwide. It was like he was the Super President of the world. I saw a visitor from Communist Europe pick up his picture and kiss it. That kind of leadership can have huge impacts on war and peace, and a general cooperativeness among nations.

There is a stark difference between JFK's way and the macho saber rattling of George W. Bush, Ronald Reagan and Richard Nixon. The "election" of George W. Bush was bad enough in the eyes of the world's population. When he was re-elected the world took a much cooler view of us. From comments I heard directly from foreign visitors, they thought U. S. citizens were going insane. Those comments were not elicited in any way by me.

John Kennedy was a volunteer officer in charge of PT-109, a small fast 3000 horsepower attack boat in WWII. It carried 4 torpedoes as it searched for Japanese ships in the Pacific. PT-109 was hit straight on and destroyed by a Japanese ship in an area used heavily for transporting supplies. Fortunately, Kennedy and most of his crew survived and kicked their way to an island while holding onto a wooden part of the wreck. They were left by the Japanese who assumed nobody would have lived through such a hit.

With no food or water on that island Kennedy swam to another island in search of food and water. After finding coconuts and water he returned and lead his crew to that island from which they were eventually rescued. He did all that while having an injured back which he had before he enlisted.

His family was a prominent wealthy Massachusetts' family which amassed a fortune from importing alcoholic beverages, like scotch, and from investments in Hollywood movies. A lot of money was also made through the New York Stock Exchange in the day before there was any regulation controlling such investments.

It was a family which suffered one tragedy after another. Many members served in the military and in political positions. Unfortunately, JFK's life was cut short when he was assassinated in Texas while serving as President.

William "Bill" Jefferson Clinton

As a young man Bill Clinton had the idea planted in his head to serve in government when on a trip to the White House he met and shook hands with

President John F. Kennedy. Bill is a Rhodes Scholar who also opposed the war in Vietnam as I did.

The French had been there fighting in Vietnam unsuccessfully for 27 years or so. They decided to end the war and become a normal country which traded with Vietnam instead of owning and controlling it. France needed the natural rubber from Vietnam in manufacturing Michelin tires. There was also oil, rice and expensive tropical woods from the former possession acquired during France's imperialistic period.

The French had always had an appreciation for America which had liberated them from German control during World Wars I and II. In the 1880's, they had given us the Statue of Liberty to help celebrate America as the world's symbol of independence, and of France and United States working together.

Tired of their long Vietnam war they told us in no uncertain terms to stay out of it. We could not win, and if we chose to start a U. S. war there it would mess up the business relations and trading they had finally been able to secure.

When President Eisenhower ignored their request, France became extremely angry, a condition which still exists decades later. "Our" attitude didn't help much either. France became a nation with a heavy 10% Muslim population.

Do you remember Republicans making the cafeteria at the Capitol take French fries off the menu? France was correct. We couldn't win no matter how much time, treasure and lives we spent there. Around 60,000 real persons from America died there. How many lost arms, legs or personalities there on the battle field? It was just another macho thing by those who believed in the Domino Theory. If Vietnam goes Communistic, all the others will, too.

That was just another baseless GOP theory which had no connection to reality. It did help defense contractors and companies add to their piles of wealth. Wars are great for profits, bad for troops and tax payers; and our image in the world.

The nations of England and Scandinavia are close to becoming Muslim. As one of the Muslim leaders in England put it, "It is just as matter of time!" I believe the Muslim religion emphasizes eradicating those who don't willingly convert to their religion.

Bing sources show Christians on Earth as having an estimated 2.2 - 2.5 billion members. That is the religion with the largest following. Muslims are second with 1.6 - 2.1 billion, or 23.4% of the Earth's population.

Some think of Islam as a religion with a set of fanatical ideas. It is a stated aim to populate the world with an overwhelming majority. I have heard Republicans on television spouting anger on not being allowed to bring more foreigners here to fill computer/internet type jobs. Those persons are mainly in the Middle East.

They will work for a quarter or a third the pay and benefits an American would cost. If Republicans would take more interest in top notch education here, and in giving up more of the massive profits taken in, we would be more competitive and inventive in the world and have less unemployment. Again, it boils back to greed - as more Muslims are allowed to come here to take our jobs- and to populate America; and set up their radical religion.

There is a huge difference in the way the religious leaders present their beliefs. With his sons' help and her mother's approval, a father's killing of his daughter because she was raped, is not close to the thinking of most Americans.

How about women's rights? We spend hundreds of billions each year to protect our country, our way of life. Why jeopardize America just to save some money? As we allow immigrants in, why aren't we more selective in admitting individuals with thinking more in line with ours? Eventually others from around the world may come around in their thinking to something closer to ours, or they can live a more segregated life as in Iran and North Korea.

Those of you who think a dominant religion in America should be given preference, be prepared to say the Pledge with "Under Allah" down the road. If that thought upsets you, you can understand why those who wrote our Constitution specifically called for a separation of church and state. Religion has many benefits for individuals and for a country, or for the world. To me religion has no place in government as our founding fathers expressed in our Constitution.

Look at the history of government led religions in the Roman Empire, in the Middle East, in England, and in so many places. Government controlled religion was disliked so strongly in England people took big risks in leaving to live a new life in America where religion was supposed to not be integrated into government.

Pushing one's religious beliefs onto another is bullying, pure and simple. When people want something, like ice cream, they don't have to be forced or bullied into accepting it.

At big risks President Clinton had two brief wars in Haiti and in Bosnia. Not one American was killed in either war. He stated what he was setting out to do, then went and did it. The ideas worked because they were well thought out, and there were no ulterior motives like creating business for defense contractors or getting oil rights.

Bill Clinton, the candidate, campaigned on many conservative ideas including changing welfare to a two year max form of support. Then he saw the ideas through, showing success every time. Republicans, who were not able to do similar things, were very frustrated with his successes, so they looked for issues to use for trashing him. Their ideas will never work because they are flawed and based on greed.

As they are now trying to do with President Obama, the GOP tried to hang the labels communist and liberal on Clinton. Neither Clinton nor Obama are left wing. If you notice Clinton and now Obama have had support even from Wall Street. A President is supposed to represent all the people. When Republicans are in charge, or even when they aren't, they are adamant about only supporting the rich. Except for just before elections, Republicans are always opposed to Social Security, Medicare, unemployment, payments to employees who have been injured on the job and anything which would help the poor or middle class.

In Congressman Ryan's recent proposed budget (MSNBC 04-09-2012)there was no evidence of shared sacrifice. First, he wanted the massive Bush tax cuts, aimed at the rich, made permanent. Of America's 22,000 millionaire/billionaires, 1500 paid ZERO TAXES. The other 20,000+ likely paid pretty close to nothing.

Over the coming 10 years Ryan wanted to cut $5.3 trillion from Medicare, a program which does not use tax payer funds. Workers fund Medicare and Social Security in their entirety. They only look broke because Republicans borrow, with the intent to never repay, any excesses at the moment.

With Veterans having huge increased needs after two wars and daily suicides Ryan proposed cutting Veterans' benefits 13%. There was 33% less for education, and at a time we need jobs and to fix a crumbling infrastructure, the committee's majority said, "25% LESS for transportation!" We pay many, many billions in fuel and road taxes into the funds to fix and increase our highway system. If those funds are "stolen," we hear, "There isn't money to do that!"

"Let's have two wars, cut taxes on the rich and not fix America; oh yeah, give free rein to banks and Wall St." That is the policy which has trickled down on all of us who work for a living and own a home for the years under Reagan, Bush and Bush. I swear, some who have lost their jobs, their homes and their retirement savings will vote for Willard. Conservative quarterback Senator Jack Kemp put it into perspective when he politely stated, "Americans have the Constitutional right to be.. wrong!"

Ryan's proposed tax corrections had two parts which stuck out in my mind the most. They were tax changes for those having one million dollars of adjusted income, and one whose adjusted income was $10,000. The millionaire would **save an additional $265,000+** while the worker with $10,000 would **pay an increased $112**. And this proposal was made during a Presidential election year, a time they lighten up.

To me a person's personal life is not my business. I may not approve of another's actions but compare Clinton's lie over a personal matter with President Reagan's continuous lying to us over national security with Iran-Contra. And in terms of spending, President Reagan left more national debt than the total of all previous Presidents combined.

With President Clinton, by the end of his second term after having balanced budgets, a $5.77 TRILLION surplus was left to the next President, George W. Bush. We all know how he spent, and spent beyond the surplus. And he spent on two major wars off the books. Bush took a $5.77 trillion surplus to around a $13 trillion debt. Bill Clinton is correct when he says Americans always hire Democrats to straighten out Republican debt fiascos.

Add a trillion dollars a year in interest to George W. Bush's train wreck, and a couple trillion to replace worn out machinery which had not been replaced by Bush. Then blame President Obama instead of the owner of the debt. It was done on purpose knowing busy people would miss the truth.

Combining trillions in lost tax income with $4 trillion in interest ($1 trillion X 4 years,) and $2 trillion to replace tanks, Patriot missiles, aircraft, over 100,000 Hummers, fuel tanker vehicles, etc., etc. - and pretty soon you are talking real money. There is no smoke and mirrors to it.

A few news journalists point out the facts to Republicans being interviewed. Those Republicans are so programmed they continue blaming President Obama even immediately after being corrected. Why isn't every viewer angered by the repeated lies? I'm thinking especially about those persons who have said they were really offended by Bill Clinton's lie. Republicans are very quick to condemn Clinton for his womanizing while married. I don't hear that item thrown into conversations when the names Dwight D. Eisenhower, George H. W. Bush, or Nelson Rockefeller are brought up. Why doesn't it matter equally? The judge involved in Clinton's attempted impeachment, was filmed leaving the courtroom and driving to a motel where he meet a woman not his wife. Let's judge each by the same standards.

President Clinton was and still is loved and respected around the world. He has dedicated his life to eradicating hunger, medical problems and illiteracy.

He and Hillary have apparently come to a conclusion in what is a private matter between them. It is not my business, nor do I believe yours. Although I acknowledge affairs do happen for various reasons, it doesn't mean I support them.

He can talk about any subject using facts and figures and keep a cool head while doing it. He always shows respect for others, even those who are attacking him. Bill was well respected by leaders around the world. They knew he would not put up with nonsense while being a good friend at the same time. He didn't try to put on a macho, "I can crush you," image.

If President Clinton could have served three or four terms, our country would be in a great position with a steady, strong economy and little unemployment today.

Barack Obama

Following the worst trashing of America's economy since The Great Depression, President Barack Obama took over a mess called The Great Recession. Two wars were still underway, the war equipment was worn out after operating from 2003 to January 2009 in sand and heat, there continued to be a trillion dollars a year just in interest on the spending for Bush's two elective wars, and budgets were jumbled from continuous off the books spending.

Jobs were disappearing from the U. S. at a rate of nearly **800,000** in the **month** prior to Obama's taking office in January 2009. The avalanche was already under way. It certainly didn't help America as President George W. Bush exported many thousands of good jobs in calculated efforts; and with Willard Romney exporting both U. S. jobs and factory machinery. Romney amassed **$250,000,000+** for his efforts in killing jobs in America. It may have been legal, but to me it certainly is not patriotic. Helping make America strong, to me, is patriotic. That is why I enlisted! I don't believe Willard enlisted. He just milked America and Americans and the results of their hard work and dedication.

He also made money setting up phony oversea's business addresses which saved companies like GE from paying any taxes on **$34 billion in profits** even though they were still operating here in America.

And in Congress Republicans actually passed a bill under President Bush requiring U. S. taxpayers to reimburse any company like GE which had to pay taxes to a foreign country - even though they paid no taxes to our federal government.

Republicans stood up strong for that bill and law, the same as they continue to do for giving $40,000,000,000 (yes, that's $40 billion) to oil companies on a continual basis. And blocking Democrats' efforts to find and recover $100 billion in missing Iraq war funds. And, did you know George W. Bush cut Veterans' benefits by billions on the very day he invaded Iraq with shock and awe? And they say we must cut costs like help to Veterans! As a Veteran I am appalled if you vote for those who show such disrespect to Veterans. I get angry as I write this!

Giving such tax breaks to companies like GE cut into the income for America as did the 12 years of Bush tax cuts mainly for the rich. Never before in American history have taxes ever been cut during a war. They have always been raised - on everybody. Payrolls are down so less revenues were coming in. America was sputtering with fewer jobs, less income and Republicans in control of both the House and the Senate.

With control by Grover Norquist and the Koch brothers, Republicans have had no backbone in stimulating the economy with infrastructure spending Shame on them and any of you who go along with that thinking. We have already paid the taxes on gasoline and Diesel fuels, and through road taxes. We need those repairs and expansions now. Repairing a bridge is way cheaper than replacing it.
And it definitely will help keep some of us from needlessly dying. You, your wife, your daughter, your son, your husband, father or mother, your aunt, uncle, nephew, niece or grandparents - or maybe some special friends. It is a given: no repairs does equal deaths.

President Obama is interrupting the steady flow toward the fascist government the rich want. Things have been going too well as Republicans gained control of the House, Senate and the Supreme Court. If only they could capture the Presidency, too. Nobody could protest anything anywhere and win, or even get heard. The dream of a government like Hitler's, of, by and for the corporations and the rich could become a reality granting them their wish, the result of their decades-long project.

"Hacking Democracy," a movie, shows just how easy it is to throw an election. The CEO of Diebold was the Republican chairperson in Ohio for George W. Bush's Presidential election. He promised Bush he would deliver Ohio, and he did.

Diebold is one of the largest manufacturers of election machines. Official cartridges for delivering election results to a county seat can be pre-programmed to split the votes any way someone wants. I suggest you watch the movie. It will blow you away because it is so simple to do.

In heavily Democratic areas in Florida George W. Bush won despite consistent high Democratic voting in previous elections, and exit polls showing Democrats winning by large margins. Diebold voting machines were used. In third world countries this is a standard for elections; but this is supposed to be America where morals are supposed to be visible. I am embarrassed for Republicans even if they are not. Imagine Castro or other dictators discussing U. S. elections. A party which will lie, deceive and cheat will do anything to get its way.

There is a distinct racist element to the Republican Party. Let me be clear in saying I do not believe every Republican is a racist. I will also state every person I have witnessed exhibiting racist words or actions are all persons associated with the Republican or Conservative Parties. I have not witnessed any Democrat being a racist. Never!

I believe Republicans especially do not want to see a Black man successful in cleaning up a horrific mess brought on by "leadership" of three white men and a Congress dominated by Republican white men.

President Obama and Democrats took on the largest dollar issue in our country, healthcare, and were the first in the one hundred year issue to come to a solution. Healthcare costs us over 16% of our GDP (gross national product.)

In other modern countries the average cost is $2500 per person per year. Our costs are $8500. Why?

Health insurance premiums are astronomical. The pharmaceutical companies have a willing stranglehold on Republicans in Congress. Competition has been circumvented. I recall a story on one drug which sold for $6.95. The price jumped to a wild price like $1600.00 "because of a shortage." That was not illegal apparently. Democratic Congressmen and women complained so vigorously the price was dropped to $695.00.

Chinese drugs can come to the U. S. directly but can't come through Canada which has a better handle on drug prices. The VA bargains for drug prices saving 40 to 70%.

Congressional Republicans specifically refuse to allow Medicare to bargain the same way. They are adamant. Remember of, by and for the fascist corporations. The Republicans won't back down, and don't appear to be embarrassed. They say they are protecting us from bad drugs.

A third thing pushing medical costs up is the privatization of hospitals and other healthcare facilities. Their prices are even more stunning.

Did you know Blue Cross/Blue Shield is a non-profit? I recall the news story around twenty years ago in which the CEO gave himself a bonus like $460,000,000 for that year. Laws which allow such make stealing legal. Every vote you give to a Republican assures a very few persons can manipulate and continue to do such things to us day in and day out.

One Republican told me Republicans had to "grab money" in those ways to get together money to provide jobs to others. I asked her if she had ever heard of 401-K's. Money paid in a fair way to employees is placed into stocks thereby raising money to back the growth of businesses. She maintained workers didn't know what they were doing. It should be left to the smart people. She equated greed to smart.

Look at what President George W. Bush and Republicans did to our country - and the world. To me they are like immature children thinking all about "me" trashing anything in their way to get what they want - money and power.

Democrats want everyone to do well, even the rich. We think people who show up and work hard helping create huge stores of profits should have a chance to share in those profits to purchase basic needs. Workers should be respected for their labors and should be able to bargain for a chunk of the pie. If they feel they aren't being treated well enough, why shouldn't they be able to say, "We're not working until we get a fair bargain?"

It is in everyone's interest to resolve issues peacefully and in advance. Problems develop when employers are not willing to share enough so workers have the resources to buy all the necessities of life. Then is when food stamps and HEAP come into play. They shouldn't be necessary. I am pretty sure workers would rather have more pay than handouts.

An employee on minimum wage doesn't earn enough to even pay for healthcare. Now that is wrong on any level. Food stamps and HEAP are corporate welfare designed to allow corporations to pay lower wages. Minimum wage doesn't equate to a sense of fair play.

Chapter 9 <u>RANDOM DAY BY DAY HAPPENINGS</u>

Some persons can be great word smiths and with a polished smile and easy going demeanor can get your attention and lead you to believe the message they want you to believe. Whatever the reasons are "news journalists" use in deciding not to challenge political figures when those persons tell known lies only encourage more of the same. That's why I have dwelled on giving you many examples instead of slick words.

When a person defies all logic and the very vision in front of his eyes, in favor of a well-constructed lie, he doesn't have much to offer society.

I have mentioned corporate welfare in various forms given to low wage earners in the form of HEAP, WIC, school lunches, etc. We taxpayers pay for what the employers are selfishly not paying.

The following is a partial list mostly of forms of corporate welfare which would be in line with the fascist beliefs of corporations as persons - "of, by and for **corporations**" as opposed to "of, by and for the **people**" as in democracy. Our country is under a much larger assault from within than from terrorists who have taken a couple of our large buildings. Our tax dollars going out as corporate welfare include:

*2008 $700,000,000,000 to banks (foreign and U. S.,) Wall St. companies and insurance companies like AIG under President George W. Bush as most were about to fold;

*2008 AIG alone received $182.5 billion. In my opinion no business should be allowed to get so big it couldn't be allowed to fail;

*6/2012 dollars to be given to NYS apple growers because frost might have killed some of their blossoms during a period of time we normally have frosts;

*6/10/2012 $96,000,000 in NYS toward hydraulic fracturing (fracking) of natural gas drilling many oppose;

*6/16/2012 NYS is adding $3,800,000 to a package totaling $28,000,000 for Amphenol Corporation, a defense contractor, in nearby Sidney, N. Y., after its plant was flooded by the Susquehanna River and ground water in 2006, and again in September 2011. I do understand NYS and local workers wanting Amphenol to remain local. This is to explain where your tax dollars go. It is about choices, and manipulative pressures.

The Delaware County Industrial Development Agency will purchase and develop a 23 acre parcel for Amphenol's use. The development includes a natural gas pipeline for miles to the new plant along with adding other utilities. There are huge tax credits involved, also. After all these expenses Amphenol is bound by a lease for only 20 years.

Corporations know they hold the trump cards especially when their party has caused unemployment to the point people will beg for a low paying job. How many of you will agree with me when I say Amphenol will make noise about leaving again when its tax credits expire?

Corporations say rewarding shareholders with profits is number one for them. Does that mean they can't work with a sense of fair play? Any high school kid can steal a kindergartener's lunch pretty easily. Is it right?
*6/16/2012 Bassett Healthcare Networks, based in Cooperstown, N. Y., will receive chunks of $301.1 million in HEAL NY grants. Twenty separate HEAL NY steps total $3 billion. The $13.7 million will be divided with $8.7 million to A. O. Fox Hospital in Oneonta, and $5 million to support building a new primary care site in Cobeskill, N. Y. Both hospitals are believed to be non-profit. These are but a few of hidden healthcare costs we all pay for.
*6/08/2012 $4,400,000 for 325 electric vehicle charging stations at various locations in NYS;
*6/08/2012 $2,200,000 to another businessman who is purchasing the Bresee's Department Store. These funds will go toward the $6,000,000 restoration and remodeling of the large Main St. building into about twenty apartments and many business locations which will be rented here in Oneonta, a small city with a State College and Hartwick College. Apartments are scarce.
I might note other public monies have been put into the revamping and partial demolition of this building already. A family which had made profits for years abandoned the building pushing the costs onto local and State taxpayers. This is a very big trend for corporations at our expense.
*The above follows city residents paying to demolish a rat infested animal feed company which yielded profits for two families for decades until they abandoned it in a similar fashion throwing all costs onto taxpayers. By comparison another city land owner owned land on which a small storage shed held his lawn mower and tools, if I remember correctly. He refused to tear the building down when the City ordered him to. It looked pretty solid and well kept to me. The City added the demolition costs to his tax bill after they had it torn down. Compare the treatment of corporations to that of an individual.

More Political Comparisons

2008 With, "Let them fail!" Romney clearly stated he wanted General Motors to fail and go out of business putting millions of workers out of work. And those were good jobs with good benefits. Candidate Barack Obama wisely knew letting our nation lose such an important industry would be a big blow to our economy for years.

President Obama's way was a proven success. Romney somehow now wants full credit for saving General Motors! This is taking his windmill status to another level. He turns into the wind no matter what his previous position. The sad thing is many Republicans will automatically believe and defend him. Republicans expect its members to be stupid lumps of pliable clay. Many comply.

General Motors, under pressures and having revamped many aspects of its business including improving its products reliability and technology, has been doing very well in its comeback. Profits are coming back fast as it performs with 5 fewer jetliners, lower wages and benefits, thousands fewer employees in the administration wing, and with corrections on lavish bonuses.

Romney wants our government to immediately sell the GM stocks taxpayers own which would result in a $16 billion loss to our government. Instead of waiting a little longer for the stocks' prices to go up, allowing great profits for taxpayers who bailed GM out, Romney wants that $16 billion to shift to rich investors. Why am I not surprised?

Republican thinking is always to figure ways to shift money to the very rich. It is a constant. Incidentally, according to television news Romney owns General Motors stocks and would therefore benefit greatly if the U. S. sold its stocks prematurely. Other rich investors would also gain a share of the $16,000,000,000 grab.

This represents a perfect example of how the rich easily add to their wealth. If Romney were President and sold those GM stocks now, it would cost every average family of four $208. Such nibbles on your dollars add up faster than you might think.

Sixteen billion is 16,000 millions. Divide the $16 billion by roughly 77,000,000 hypothetical families of four. The large bulk of those dollars would end up in the pockets of just a few thousand rich stock investors. Such a sale would be just a blip on the news if it even appeared.

A hypothetical newscast: "Today the U. S. sold its GM stock it acquired when it bailed out General Motors. All funds loaned to GM were recovered except $16 billion. Now in sports, Yankee star, Derek Jeter, hit a grand slam which firmly locked the Yankees into the number one position in their league." Such ripoffs are so common they aren't even news.

How much would this fake GM news mean to the average citizen who is busy working and raising a family, maybe someone who vaguely knew his tax dollars bailed out one of our country's core businesses? The expression, "A little knowledge is a dangerous thing," applies, for if everyone knew something was going on, there would be a change.

The rich want dumb voters, and Republicans in at least 26 states are trying to set up barriers intended to restrict voting by Democrats, especially by minorities. They claim elections are being thrown because of improper voting by Democrats. Counting both parties there have been three questionable individual votes during the past ten years nationwide, and they all had to do with absentee ballots. Perhaps more time should be utilized to figure why Diebold machines give contradictory results; and the amazing sudden change in districts voting heavily Democratic for decades going to Republicans now with Diebold machines. No person outside Diebold is allowed to see the insides of or work on any Diebold machine.

With straight faces Republicans continue wanting to require particular picture i. d.'s. Cell phones now capture scenes where white Republicans are not even asked for an i. d. while minority voters who are known and have voted using a signature for years are not allowed to vote. Military picture i. d.'s held by active minority servicemen have been denied as proper proof. In some cases the "proper" i. d. can cost $100 or more plus time and travel. Many voters, especially in cities, don't own a car or a driver's license. These irregularities in voting procedures were supposed to have been cleared up many years ago with major legislation. How do you suppose a very far right wing Supreme Court Republican majority would rule on such voting irregularities? In Citizens United they totally disregarded the Constitution allowing corporations, foreign or American, to secretly donate any amount of money in any election.

Republican Governor Scott in Florida is going all out to make sure restrictions work in a state very important in Presidential elections. Such restrictions are huge bites weakening our democratic form of government.

Under President George W. Bush, banks, Wall St. companies and insurance companies like AIG were allowed to run wild. As anyone with a brain would know such a house of cards will fall sooner or later. In desperation, Bush and Secretary Paulson addressed Americans saying a three page $700 billion bailout was needed immediately to prevent a total collapse.

As it turned out we bailed out foreign owned banks including Citibank purportedly owned in most part by the dictator of Saudi Arabia. Unless AIG made a recent repayment, we taxpayers still have $182.5 billion loaned to a company which plays fast and loose with other peoples' money. Their license should be yanked, and their policies distributed to other companies. They should be made to fold as Lehman Brothers was forced to.

Corporate welfare usually is given out in huge numbers so they add up very quickly. Monies shelled out as corporate welfare far exceed all forms of money used to support poor people in the United States; and the numbers of people helped is vastly larger in poor people welfare cases.

Which makes more sense to support, someone who works hard for low pay who stumbles and needs basic materials for living; or a company which either doesn't need help, or has taken wild and illegal risks?

6/06/2012 A man owning area dog kennels, who faces felony charges, now is refusing to pay bills of nearly $100,000 for medical care, housing and feeding of numerous animals which were in horrible condition. He has said, "No." to allowing the animals to be adopted. Who will pay the bills for animals picked up by a court order? Add to that the costs of the trial(s) and the likely incarceration of him for several years? I believe his business is a corporation.

6/02/2012 Grover Norquist has been successful in getting 238 of 242 Republicans to sign a pledge they will not vote for any tax increases on the rich. He includes allowing the 12 years of Bush tax cuts to automatically die to be a tax increase. Only 4 Republicans had the backbone to stand up to the well financed Norquist machine. Republicans don't allow independent thinking, so all fall in line like a bunch of sheep. Directives come from what the rich say needs to get done. It is actually sad. They think so little of themselves. If elected I would like to think I could come up with some good ideas others might support. Magic money flows to those who follow the narrow directives.

Below is a June 2 and 3, 2012 "IN OUR OPINION" editorial reprinted courtesy of **The Daily Star**, Oneonta, N. Y. entitled "Rejecting tax pledge would ease D. C. gridlock."

Several Republican candidates for Congress have made news recently by refusing to sign conservative lobbyist Grover Norquist's anti-tax pledge. Since 1986, Norquist has pressured lawmakers to sign his Taxpayer Protection Pledge, in which lawmakers vow to oppose tax increases of any kind. Of the 242 Republicans serving in the House, 238 have signed the pledge, including Rep. Chris Gibson, R-Kinderhook. To his credit, Rep. Richard Hanna, R-Barneveld, has not.

But of the 25 leading candidates being promoted by the National Republican Congressional Committee, at least one-third have indicated they are unwilling to sign the pledge.

The notion that Norquist's pledge is a sincere defense of taxpayers should have been rejected a long time ago, as the myriad loopholes that exist in the tax code can't be closed without violating the pledge.

Such loopholes benefit some taxpayers more than others. According to a Bloomberg report this week, one out of every 189 taxpayers earning more than $200,000 annually - 10,800 households in all, paid no income taxes at all last year.

But in the Norquist pledge, no credits or deductions can be eliminated "unless matched dollar-for-dollar by further reducing tax rates." That's what former Republican state Sen. Richard Tisei of Massachusetts was worried about when he refused to sign the pledge.

"If there's a loophole that can be closed that ends up generating additional revenue that can be used specifically to pay down the national debt, I'm not going to lose sleep," Tisei said to the Washington Post last week. "And I don't want to be bound by the pledge not to close it."

Pennsylvania state Rep. Scott Perry echoed Tisei's concerns, saying he was disappointed when all the GOP presidential candidates said in a debate last fall they would have rejected a deal during last year's debt-ceiling standoff that would have matched $10 in spending cuts for every $1 in tax increases. Norquist's pledge also precludes the plan suggested by the 2010 National Commission on Fiscal Responsibility and Reform, which called for a formula of 85 percent spending cuts and 15 percent tax increases.

Former Wyoming Sen. Alan Simpson, a Republican, vented his frustration with Norquist to CNN's Fareed Zakaria last weekend.

"For heaven's sake, you have Grover Norquist wandering the Earth in his white robes saying that if you raise taxes one penny, he'll defeat you," he said. "He can't murder you. He can't burn your house. The only thing he can do to you, as an elected official, is defeat you for re-election."

Or, as Norquist's waning popularity suggests, he might drag down your re-election prospects. Politics is based on compromise, and Norquist's brand of obstructionism makes governance nearly impossible.

While scanning newspapers I have not been looking through the sports' section so I may have missed some corporate welfare there. A few years back Oneonta had a Yankees' farm team which operated from a rebuilt stadium in Neawha Park owned by the City of Oneonta (say: own ee on ta.) It is the field Derek Jeter played on prior to being moved up to the majors. Yankee owner, Steinbrenner, was a very wealthy man yet demanded Oneonta taxpayers spend $250,000 to replace the topsoil on the field. The arrogance of the rich is unbelievable. His team used the field for free.

5/22/2012 An applied science campus in New York City was set up for training employees for companies like Google. At least $100 million of costs were supported through taxes as such companies produce multiple billions in profits.

5/15/2012 Democrats in New York State were trying to get minimum wage up to $8.25/hour from the current $7.25. 78% of residents want the minimum wage raised; 17% are against it. In Albany, Republicans gave a resounding, "No!' to the bill. Score zero for of, by and for the people (democracy,) and one for the corporations (fascism.)

5/09/2012 The Superfund was set up with a huge number of billions in taxpayer funds to pay for cleanup of messes almost always made by corporate polluters. In many cases the polluters were well aware of the dangers yet continued polluting anyway.

One Schenectady, N. Y. company, General Electric, dumped polychlorinated biphenyls (PCB's) into the Hudson River north of Schenectady and Albany. The dredging and removal of 2,000,000 cubic yards of contaminated materials will take over 4 years and over $1 billion to accomplish.

General Electric used our infrastructure as it profited $13.12 billion last year (2011,) yet pays no U. S. taxes thanks to work done by Romney and Congressional Republicans. Bain Capital made huge profits setting up phony unmanned offices in the Cayman Islands and elsewhere in slick moves to remove corporations from having any U. S. tax liabilities.

I, for one, feel a corporation using our roads, bridges, courts, airports, etc. should pay its fair share in taxes. Why should you and I have to pick up the costs incurred by corporations? Why aren't farmers angered by these free riders?

Chapter 10 **WHERE DOES THE MONEY GO?**

Suppose **you wrote every government check**. What would you find out?

The United States Postal Service...All USPS costs are paid for through its own revenue stream. NO TAX DOLLARS ARE INVOLVED!

Social Security -NO TAX DOLLARS ARE INVOLVED!...Premiums paid into this insurance program cover all costs. It has trillions in surpluses currently which should be in a lockbox. Social Security, Medicare and the U. S. Postal Service should not even be in our general fund budgets.

Medicare - again, NO TAX DOLLARS ARE INVOLVED...All costs are paid from premiums paid in by workers.

National Defense...the largest payments from taxes have to do with our national defense; troops, training, housing, medical costs, food, clothing, travel, retirements, equipment, parts and repairs, bases, Veterans' care and benefits, research, defense contractors and other things we can't imagine. Cost overruns are normal. There is little verification on the battlefield about whether or not goods or services are delivered, or if they met specifications. Vice President Dick Cheney was CEO of Halliburton, a war services and oil services company, which with several subsidiaries, were paid multiple billions from involvement in wars in Afghanistan and Iraq. Halliburton billed for twice the number of meals it served. Troops have said Halliburton's slop was so bad they ate emergency rations instead.

I recall reading the Bush administration had Halliburton buy thousands of foreign made pickups for use in Iraq. We were charged three times what we as private citizens would buy them for, plus delivery charges to Iraq.

Well over $100 billion in funds appropriated for equipment intended to protect our troops, like vests and armor plating, disappeared from our treasury. Republicans either had 100% complete control, or had President Bush's veto. Democrats made many efforts to find and recover the funds. Without fail they were blocked every single time. Our troops went with "what we have, not what we wish for," according to Secretary of Defense, Donald Rumsfeld.

Bush did two things to make his administration look better than it was. He put all the war costs off the books so the spending didn't show up in any budget. Secondly, he didn't replace any of the worn out equipment pushing those costs forward onto President Obama. Bush left us in a very compromised state while he was "President."

Throughout U. S. history taxes on every income level were raised, that is until W. Bush took us into two wars based on lies. Instead of raising taxes to pay for his wars, he set in motion 12 years of huge tax breaks mainly for the rich. The spending by Republicans who were 100% in charge killed the $5.77 trillion surplus and added trillion after trillion to our national debt. There was no balking by Republicans as they made the debt increases almost automatic. Their debt is so high the interest is right next to a trillion dollars a year on their spending just on the wars.

I estimated Bush's Iraq War will cost at least $4 trillion plus trillions in interest. Some have challenged me on that figure, but a couple months ago Republican Presidential candidate, Ron Paul, from Texas, used the exact same figure. Care for Veterans and replacing equipment will run the register for several years. You really need to Google Project of the New American Century and spend some time reading it. You will understand a lot more about why lies were made to get us into a war in Iraq. I guarantee if you had a friend or family member killed or maimed there, you will be angry.

Major corporate welfare

Another type of spending you'd be writing checks for would be for big items like bailing out 1043 thrift banks for $153 billion. There were Bush names on directors doors of some of those thrifts that failed; and many unpaid loans. It would take a book as thick as "War and Peace" to write about all the scamming which went on there. It seems the more brazen and crooked a person is, the more people will vote for and support them.

Bush's $700 billion to bail out crooks who took investors monies and made bets they knew should fail, isn't much different from Madoff's scheming. Madoff finally got jail; the bankers and Wall St. got the royal treatment - bailed out with our tax money. By the way, Bernie Madoff was twice reported as running a scam. The Bush administration didn't want to hear about such things.

Then there was President Obama's $787 billion bailout of the auto industry, in his stimulus bill. It did create jobs, maintain jobs and saved the U. S. auto industry. It is making it and will be stronger than ever. General Motors and Chrysler are both well on their way repaying the bailout funds.

In the past, Chrysler was bailed out and to their credit paid it off early with interest to our treasury. We actually made a profit.

FDR stimulated the economy with the CCC (Civilian Conservation Corp) building parks, planting trees, etc. and in projects like the TVA (Tennessee Valley Authority) which continues generating electricity eighty years later. Trees planted have been being used for making paper, and the parks are used for fun and nearby cheap vacations.

Tax credits are the same as cash when a business goes to pay its taxes. Such credits are in the billions. President W. Bush gave $40 billion in cash to airlines after 9-11. Why? NY farmers will get money because frost got some of their blossoms. When will this nonsense stop? I am not anti-farmer.

After Bush gave the airlines $20 billion plus $20 billion he then purchased hundreds of millions in flight tickets which were never used. He would not even let troops use them on a standby basis. I can imagine he got some of it donated back in campaign contributions - or in some other ways.

Is that abuse of office? The media don't carry such news very often especially on Fox and on Clearwater.

Sell Some Infrastructure

Another deal for corporations is to build something like a roadway, make sure it has everything necessary, then sell it cheap to a private business. New York GOP Governor Pataki tried to sell our NYS Thruway in a sweetheart deal. He also illegally moved residents from a mental institution into buildings owned by his sister's husband paying very high rates, and without providing required services. Again it was a fairly quiet deal.

For at least two decades Republicans have been trying to make the Post Office a private business. In 2006, Republicans passed a law Bush signed requiring the Post Office to bank enough funding to pay all retirements to be paid out during the next 70 to 75 years. Some who will be receiving pensions during that time aren't even born yet.

The instant cure to money for the Post Office would be to start charging businesses the same as we are charged. Charging 5 cents to deliver a package you or I would pay $5 to 7 for is insane, unfair to us and just wrong. This has been going on for a long, long time.

Now if you were to be a buyer of the Post Office wouldn't you feel great knowing you would not have to set aside any funds to pay any pensions for 75 years? And if it's anything like some corporations the buyer may accidentally lose some or all of those funds. Oops!

Republicans take years, even several decades in setting up such deals. More corporate welfare in the pipeline.

Miscellaneous Government Costs

Then there are buildings, parks, monuments, airports, Amtrak, prisons, canals, roadways to build, repair and staff, all kinds of things. Throw in police and firemen, too. You'd be writing lots of checks.

Education

Who makes the most noise about needing employees who have basic skills? Computer software and hardware companies need employees with advanced skills. All corporations want and need educated employees. An employee without skills is slow or non-productive, or makes costly mistakes. Education, an expensive item to pay for, benefits the individual and the corporation, and humanity in general. We hope custodians and other employees in hospitals, for instance, have a broad understanding of infections and the need of washing hands and cleanliness in general. Our lives could be in the balance.

Basic math may help both but who benefits from knowing trigonometry? My point here is corporations and employers benefit proportionately higher from education. You would expect they would support education more. Imagine a corporation trying to open and run a factory in a totally backward nation.

As a teacher I have seen universal professionalism among my peers. Pay is ever so slightly better now but few teachers even earn the average income in the United States at the same time they are paying off college loans. And teachers are professionals. Imagine a doctor, dentist or lawyer not being able to pay his or her bills.

Many parents have trouble controlling their children. I imagine they would not be willing candidates to take on the job of being a teacher. This is not a putdown of parents; instead it is a recognition of skills and abilities teachers seem to have naturally.

Right wing persons against public employees try to make citizens anti-teacher saying we get huge pay and retirements. I retired with eighteen years of service and was told my retirement was to be $88 a month. Laws from Albany had moved me from Tier 1 to Tier 4. I found out I could legally make them restore my position to Tier 1, so I was able to get a retirement higher than $88. My retirement now is in the range one would pay as a car payment. It is a total lie for politicians to rail on teachers as living a high life.

My pay ranged from $5200 a year to $18,020. That $18,020 was that high because I tutored for the school, was the school's only substitute bus driver, and was the Ski Club advisor.

With the use of lies Republicans in Albany have since introduced a Tier 5 and a Tier 6. I can't imagine how small those retirement checks will be. Unless a person has access to separate wealth he or she will live a life in poverty as a teacher unless you teach in New York City. From a financial point of view and from what my family and I went through when living on my teacher's pay, I would advise anyone not to go into teaching. You are a third class citizen under the control of mostly Republican school board members. It is a sad commentary on America and its priorities. A good teacher can be the very person who assures your son or daughter gets on and stays on a good course in life. How much is that worth?

I had to leave teaching to work at jobs (highway construction and factory quality control) in order to pay off my bills. While teaching I was never able to purchase a house.

Did you know **the United States holds the 25th position regarding education in the world?**

Medical Care

Now let's go to medical care of persons from birth to 65. 16% of our GDP (Gross National Product) goes to medical care; $8500/person/year. Other countries with much better healthcare spend $2500 a year. According to the World Health Report **the U. S. ranks 37th in the world when it**

comes to healthcare. 37th! The greatest country ever! And the one which spends $8500 a year per person! Someone surely has priorities wrong!

The ownership of this lies completely in the hands of Republicans who assure you will pay the highest in premiums as they protect insurance companies, and the highest prices for drugs as they write into law we cannot bargain for competitive drug prices. At every level corporations are protected and their profits enhanced as in the following case. A cancer patient was provided with two packages of sealed drugs said to be worth well over $2000. They were placed into a refrigerator unopened for about 8 days. After the patient passed on a medical professional said she needed to destroy the unopened medicines in front of the family. They were still 100% in code,.

Asked why not let someone else use these, especially a poor patient, her answer was, "Laws were written to assure their destruction. They could only be used if Medicaid had paid for them." Does anyone else see an element of sick behavior in such a greedy law?

At 65, most who have worked enough time and paid in to Medicare can register for benefits. Medicare has thousands of scammers bilking the program on a daily basis especially in Florida.

Again, Republicans will not allow Democrats to put teeth into the Medicare language to stop scammers, put them in prisons and to recover the multiple billions stolen. There is nothing in the law allowing Medicare or any agency to stop the scammers.

In return for their name and Social Security number, homeless or poor are fed a meal and given enough money for a bottle of wine. The scammer then buys multiple wheel chairs, electrically operated chairs and numerous items using those names and Social Security numbers. Medicare must then pay under the current writings. If the solvency of Medicare is challenged, it is because of the scammers. Republicans want the program to die so they want scammers to continue. Governor Jeb Bush went out his way to help a man, believed to be a Mafia person, set up to take off with over $300,000,000 in Medicare funds. The man's Medicare insurance company was paid by Medicare, but he didn't pay the providers.

Do they know accounts and verifications can be set up? With laws blocked by the GOP no accountability or arrests can be made. Most people would look at this as lunacy. Yet numerous voters allow these "representatives" to stay in office.

Dr. Phil says you can tell certain persons are lying any time you see their lips moving. Because Republicans vote every time as a solid block, and vote against things which seem so sane to most of us, there is not much chance I will ever vote for any Republican. We really need a solid front to save America from fascists and from other such affronts against things most of us consider important like Social Security and Medicare, and our Constitution.

I can tell you since I have had Medicare (started last year at age 69) I have been given run-arounds you wouldn't believe from the corporate insurers. The companies fight everything starting out saying, "This isn't a covered item," even though it is explicit in the booklet. A three-way lengthy phone call with an insurance company person, a Medicare person and me left it at the point we all readily agreed I was definitely covered, and that there would be no more blocking from that minute. It wasn't so an hour later, and it wasn't so the next day.

In almost two years I have received less than $300 in benefits so we're not talking huge claims. A credit card payment was required for last January (2012,) for my portion of the premiums. They told me bank deductions would be started in February, yet immediately deducted a second payment for January. It still has not been repaid to me in any form. The companies are not afraid to do whatever they want. They are in the good hands of the GOP. A rejection received today states, "date of service is after patient's coverage with (the company) ended. Therefore, this claim is denied." Hello, you are taking my premiums every month! The carriers want to beat you down and escape paying. Why do they ask why there are regulations?

A person with medical needs has a few choices if he isn't paid enough to have healthcare insurance. As many people do he can go without getting the care even if it is urgent. In many times the person simply gets worse and dies. Being sick, he may not have a good handle on his options or may become depressed and not care what happens. In my mind I hope America is a bigger country than to want that to happen.

He or she likely doesn't have money to pay the bills. He can try to pay it off over time while being turned into the credit bureau, he can rob someone to pay the bill, he can ask for help under Hill-Burton Act and be ignored, or he can apply for Medicaid. Such a low income likely makes him eligible. None of the choices is appealing.

Most people want a good job with a living wage so they can be responsible and pay their bills. It is humiliating especially if he has a family and can't come close to meeting his family's needs. There can't be much pride.

Sooner or later everyone needs medical help. Persons knowing there can be big profits involved use peoples' illnesses to advance their wealth. It is that greed which takes medical costs from $2500 to $8500. The $6000 is pure greed with a price tag. Other countries find profits in $2500.

This is a problem which has existed for decades. Healthcare has been a controversial issue kicking around for over 100 years. Until President Obama, President Clinton had been the only President to take the issue on in a big way. President Obama and Democrats have been trying to resolve medical cost problems but are put down with a huge campaign as their plan tries to get a handle on the high costs which allow huge, usury profits. Republicans don't have a plan. Their profits have been so predictable and easy. They just don't want to give up the money!

Why are Republicans talking about the increased costs of healthcare under the Affordable Care Act when there have been no increased costs? If it will upset a voter and gain a vote for a Republican, the lie was worth it.

We have constantly been led to believe health insurance premiums must be high because the hospitals and health providers charge so much. A hospital stay bill may be presented as "$100,000." How surprised would you be to hear the hospital typically gets a payment of around $5000 as full payment for that $100,000 bill from the insurance company?

With the average healthcare policy cost at around $14,500 in 2010, you likely have been getting a warped sense of value from your health plan. In 30 years your premiums are $435,000 at $14,500 annually. Even if you had an expensive case like a cancer situation, you probably will never come close to a 100% return on your insurance.

Taking a wild guess at age 70 my approximation would be I have not received over $10,000 in benefits from health insurance coverage, even including what was covered for family members, too. Except for extreme cases which do exist out there, I think my case is typical.

We pay one sixth of our gross earnings into healthcare premiums because we have to. We need healthcare programs which are owned by the premium payers on the order of credit unions. We could mess up for a period of time and still have lower rates and better service, and hopefully, less runaround by being a part owner of the insurance company as a credit union member is of the credit union.

Many countries have already improved their healthcare and at a fraction of the cost by having national healthcare. Some say in a few cases medical care is delayed. I haven't researched that and I am not necessarily supporting that. I just don't know.

The Affordable Care Act leaves it up to each person to get coverage where he wants to but it will be like auto insurance - you would be required to have at least a basic policy. Why should I be made to pay for your heart surgery or your cancer care when it is a given you will probably have healthcare issues during your life. Making me pay for the care of others violates my rights to a degree.

Those who smoke, drink and eat high cholesterol diets have the rights to do that - just don't set me up as your payer when your life style catches up to you. We need to balance your rights against mine.

Here are some spending items that come to mind.

For a little perspective - the U. S. annual gross budget is $3.8 trillion. From memory I believe under President Johnson it was $99 billion.

$ 153,000,000,000 thrift banks' massive thefts under GHWBush & Reagan
    700,000,000,000 banks, Wall St., insurance companies GWBush
     40,000,000,000 oil companies subsidies under insistent Republicans
    100,000,000,000+ missing Iraq War funds investigations blocked by GOP
  4,000,000,000,000+ Bush's elective 2003 Iraq War, planned in 1997
    787,000,000,000 bailout auto industry (most repaid) + stimulus Obama
     40,000,000,000 airlines 20+20 GWBush
    125,000,000,000 Exxon's spill still not paid GWB interfered for XOM
    ???,000,000,000 Superfund to clean up corporate pollution
    ???,000,000,000 Paying pensions for corporations which "lost" the funds

Welfare for the needy

Just the first eight recent items above add up to $5.945 trillion. Oil companies, banks, airlines, Wall St., insurance companies, auto companies - all tugging at the treasury's udders.

In good times corporations believe in free enterprise/capitalism. In bad times they believe in socialism.

Chrysler, then known as Cerberus Capital Management, had been cleaned out by Dan Quayle in the same moves Romney did with Bain Capital. They stripped out and sold any valuable parts, then left the underfunded company and employees to flounder and fail. Chrysler was already in a weak state as Quayle added to his wealth. Somehow he and Romney must feel this is a way to strengthen America. Or did they not give a damn about the company, the employees or America?

To be fair General Motors was trying to come back from a time when quality had slipped to the point foreign companies were eating their lunch. GM did make huge profits but was top heavy with high paid administrators, and it had 9 jet aircraft, 5 of which were luxury.

Normally huge profits would cover such expenses, that is until the GOP and President George W. Bush's policies and spending crashed our economy to the point nobody would buy cars. GM suffered from the decline under President George W. Bush, not necessarily from its own doing.
And so did workers who lost their jobs, their homes and their retirements. Those who never would have thought it possible were now using food stamps and drawing unemployment. Aside from such temporary bad luck every society has a number of people who are injured, sick or for whatever reason are unable to work and provide for themselves. We are a compassionate nation with an abundance of wealth, and as we help poor nations with necessities, we do the same to our own unfortunate citizens.

Corporate welfare is given out every day. Republicans deny it but corporate welfare dwarfs the amounts given to our own needy persons.

President Clinton campaigned on and accomplished a two year limit for most people to be on the public dole. None of us approve of intentional free loaders. So tell me why a company like Exxon Mobil, which shows profits of $50 billion a year, should continue to receive a large portion of $40 billion on a regular basis! Republicans fight big battles to keep the oil companies on welfare! Another form of corporate welfare is Republicans as a block writing into law there can be no price negotiations on drug prices, negotiations which would save Medicare 40 to 70% on hundreds of billions of dollars of drug purchases.

Chapter 11 **BATHROOM READER STUFF**

Marriage advice from David Gray
*find someone who moves automatically when music plays
*find someone who turns and helps a baby when it cries
*find someone who is at least 25 (full brain development)

HP printer always out of ink?

Put opaque tape over the writing at the spot where you push the cartridge into place.

A "reader" then can't read the information. Use up all your "empty" cartridges, then buy another brand. I will buy no HP product after having to replace the cartridges 7 times in the first year while using only about 100 sheets of paper on one side. Although they did not admit to programming them to "run out of ink," HP paid a settlement in the 9 figures (at least 100 million.) You could get a certificate for one or two dollars good toward HP purchases if you participated in the suit. Buy no products once a company uses you!

In 2006, then again last September 2011, our area suffered from flooding, some from ground water from rain and some from the Susquehanna River swelling chasing residents out of their homes. The devastation was horrible. It continued into New England where most people lived in the valleys of steep mountains. Each time FEMA was here helping people with a fraction of the damage. I mention infrastructure many times. People are unemployed and construction equipment lays dormant during the worst economic climate since the The Great Depression in 1929.

President Obama has called for Congress to fund infrastructure work which could include making earthen barriers or even barriers made from driving metal sections into the ground. Many people just abandoned their homes. In Binghamton the flooded homes are being purchased (by local and State dollars?) and are being demolished and made into parks.

With a horrendous Republican economy Binghamton now has about 30,000 citizens, down from 85,000. Financially, they are not in a good situation to be buying up and demolishing so many homes. It also dries up a good chunk of the tax base. Fifteen years ago Binghamton was the number one NYS location to obtain a good paying job. Presidents do make a difference.

If Republicans would not be so emphatic in not doing anything to improve our economy because it would enhance President Obama's chance to be re-elected, barriers could have been built under a stimulus for less money than FEMA paid out to people as a partial help from being flooded. And all those homes now abandoned and demolished could still be there for families to live in and pay taxes on. The technology isn't new. They kept the ocean out in the Netherlands for centuries.

The U. S. is in "stupid" mode as the GOP continues to play politics. Insanity trumps sanity and what is right. You are an important part of the cure. You can tell others (don't let Republicans bully you - be truthful and steady,) and you can get out there and vote. **Things will not get better on their own.** This has been a downhill run especially since Reagan.

George H. W. Bush said the Reagan's "Trickle down on me" theory was "Voodoo economics." He was exactly correct yet bought into telling the whole country it is the perfect economic model. It hasn't worked for anyone since 1980 except for the very rich.

President Clinton certainly departed from that model and we all saw the results; great economy, jobs and a $5.77 trillion surplus with balanced budgets.

The more regressive taxes we have, the less taxes have to be collected from the rich. Taking an 8 to 9.5% tax on most all of our purchases is a huge regressive tax. The rich buy yachts, airplanes, cars, etc. under a business name paying no tax. They are "used in the production of a good or service." The process is called tax shifting. We pay sales taxes on almost 100% of our income which is the opposite of what the rich do. Even their credit cards come from a tax exempt unit.

A local man, now deceased, owned a small, local railroad and a multi-million dollar mansion on The Glimmerglass (Cooperstown Lake) in Cooperstown. It was a "non-profit" and paid no school, town, county or any other tax on those items. He entertained the New York governor and others. To me this is nothing but abuse.

We would do much better if everyone was treated the same. Get rid of such nonsense. Blue Cross/Blue Shield is also a non-profit paying no taxes. The CEO gave himself a $460 million bonus around 12 to 20 years ago. He is as poor as the oil companies drawing from the $40 billion subsidies.

U.S. Trainees include Fidel Castro, Ho Chi Minh, Noriega and Osama bin Laden.
Dick Cheney and Donald Rumsfeld were guests of or had business dealings with Saddam Hussein as evidenced in pictures shaking hands with broad smiles.
Osama bin Laden was trained in the U. S. A. as an engineer for building (or destroying) skyscraper buildings.

When our current Republicans in Congress tried to enact a law requiring forced vaginal probes on women as part of their continued attack on women, female members of Congress put in for an amendment which would require men to have a rectal prostate check every time they had a Viagra prescription filled and refilled.

"Ryan's Budget" 3/27/2012 CNN/C-SPAN... The Republican budget chaired by Paul Ryan was announced. It called for the Bush Tax Cuts to become permanent. A person being taxed on income over $1 million would save $265,000. On earnings of $10,000 an earner would pay an additional $112.

Twenty-two stock market persons with an aggregate $27 billion in earnings/profits would pay 0% to 14.9% while working persons would pay nearly 30%.

Medicare would be gutted as the elderly would be given vouchers which would expire. Any costs above the vouchers would be on the patient. Medicare, which is not supported by taxes, would continue to be plundered by Republicans through their "borrowing process." Funds are cut on the handicapped, cut on infrastructure spending, which is desperately needed for safety and for jobs, and $30 million will be given to Delta Airlines to help it with fuel costs and other items too numerous to mention. With "We can't afford all these things!" having been said, how do Republicans reconcile these generous giveaways? For 12 years, so far, our treasury has lost trillions in income because of the out and out xxxxxx Bush tax cuts which basically shovel money into the pockets of the rich.

Where do earnings go? Since 2001, 93% of earnings have gone to the top 1%; 7% has gone to 99%. These figures are normally in line with fascist or dictatorship countries according to this CNN or C-Span news showing.

An Atlanta get together At an Atlanta get together funded by the Koch brothers Republican Supreme Court judges mingled with Republican governors, the Adelsons, Karl Rove, David Koch, Charles Koch and others in an extreme right wing gathering. Is there any doubt in how 5 of the 9 persons above the law will vote?

More Supreme Court The Supreme Court heard a case regarding the Affordable Care Act in March, 2012. "Judge" Thomas refused to recuse himself although in one year alone his wife was paid over $500,000 as a lobbyist against the Affordable Care Act. In his 6 years on the Supreme Court bench Thomas has yet to make one comment about anything. Also note Thomas did not report the extreme conflict even on the forms requiring such reporting of conflicts. That is real arrogance.

Romney five decades late on foreign policy On April 2, 2012, candidate Romney thought he would show up President Obama by issuing a statement about foreign policy. To the world he announced Russia was our number one enemy. He was about 5 decades late. I was embarrassed for him. He wants to be President and apparently doesn't know much more about the world than Sarah Palin. This is your typical Republican candidate. Scary, isn't it?

Add to that he and John McCain both want the U. S. to invade Syria, another Arab country. Here are two more examples of Republicans wanting to be macho and go to war at the drop of a hat to waste your money and your children's lives and treasure. What is wrong with Arab countries having influence on each other? They don't listen to us. The U. S. is not liked over there and we ARE NOT THE WORLD'S POLICE!

As I was typing this on a Sunday night, other Republican mouth pieces were on television chiding President Obama for not sending our military into Syria to take out their dictator who continues to kill thousands of Syria's citizens while blaming a rebel group. This is a demonstration of Republicans thinking they are the smart ones, the ones who will flex their muscles and settle every little problem in the world by committing the lives and treasure of others. If they are so interested in the well being of people over there, why aren't they interested in the starving children here? Why don't they care about seeing people in the U. S. get the medical care urgently needed? They just like to go into wars! It makes them feel powerful. And the profits are big.

I am glad President Obama hasn't sent our troops there. I opposed sending our troops to Iraq and Afghanistan except to specifically get bin Laden. We are not going to change a culture thousands of years old and based on their religion. The ones we are helping are now starting to kill our troops. America is disliked. The leader of Afghanistan and his family are not only skimming money from the U. S., they continue growing poppies and selling drugs around the world especially in the U. S.

How about Romney and McCain showing their enthusiasm by purchasing their own rifles and going over on there on their own to Syria? I don't think that's going to happen. They always want to volunteer others to go to die!

Super-sizing Despite the layoffs of U. S. airport security people, food and drug inspectors, toy inspectors, and Securities and Exchange agents while calling for a smaller government, President George W. Bush added more public employees than any U. S. President ever.

President G. W. Bush and General Michael V. Hayden brought treason charges against a U. S. employee who tried to cut wasteful spending by changing war contractors. He had changed contractors away from Bush and Cheney's friends. The same man became aware of unConstitutional searches of Americans. He reported it to Congress.

Martha Stewart is a licensed stock broker. She was arrested, tried and convicted on insider trading. She is a registered Democrat. Not one Republican has even been arrested from all the stock market crimes which occurred between 2001 and 2009 when George W. Bush was President. Maybe investigations will bring some arrests soon.

Jobs' Bills **Since President Obama took office as President in January 2009, Republicans have not presented Congress with any job creation bills. None!**

Governor Rick Perry Paraphrased: "There should be no FEMA, no Social Security, or stimulus money." He boasted about creating jobs in Texas then had to admit those jobs were only possible because of stimulus dollars sent to him from President Obama. Caught in the web he stated, "I'll create more jobs if President Obama would just send me more taxpayer stimulus money!"

Passing the previous record set by former Governor George W. Bush, Rick Perry had executed 234 MORE persons than any governor had ever executed in the United States. Almost every one was a minority. He replaced 3 board members when they spoke about freeing an innocent man... who was not released.

The Royal Family from Saudi Arabia The Royal Family stayed in a gated community in Sarasota, Florida. Just before 9-11 three of the 19 hijackers visited them in Sarasota. On August 30th, the Royal Family "abruptly went back to Saudi Arabia." It was the dictators wife who had written checks to the hijackers for flying lessons, food, apartments, etc. The story said these facts are documented including copies of her checks. Other hijackers had visited San Diego to receive money for flying lessons. The Saudis there left the U. S. just before 9-11. Keep in mind this family was friends with the Bush family, even business partners. Am I the only person bewildered about the free passage for the dictator's family; and the only plane allowed in the air flying the bin Laden family out of the U. S. courtesy of President George W. Bush?
President G. W. Bush refused to allow use of pictures of him hugging and kissing the Saudi dictator. Why were those criminals put into custody if Bush had the above information?

Defense Costs During the past ten years defense costs for the U. S. are up 40% not counting the Iraq and Afghanistan Wars which were "off the books."

50,000 Factories Closed During the President George W. Bush administration 50,000 U. S. factories closed **exporting 5,500,000 jobs.** Super patriot Willard Romney was responsible for many of those job loses as he piled up $250,000,000+ in easy profits as he created jobs - out of the country. Many who lost their jobs because of him are still quite angry.

Am I wrong in thinking we are supposed to support OUR COUNTRY?

Mellon Bank Sued New York State's Attorney General sued Mellon Bank of New York for using the lowest figure for the day in rewarding currency investors instead of the closing figure? Which investment houses can be trusted? They complain about regulations. More follow through regulations are necessary, not fewer. Investment companies should be likened to vacuum cleaners at distilleries; or maybe a gambling casino. You will not beat the house. What will the penalty be - a warning?

Home Ownership From January 2001 through January 2009 home ownership dropped from 70% to 65.1%, the biggest drop since the Great Depression. In on-going scams, banks hired people at minimum wage, according to one of them, to sign retroactively, names of other people continuously all day long. Those signatures then allowed foreclosures. It was all illegal.

Four Dead in Ohio Acting out President Nixon's anger, National Guard troops on the Kent State Campus aimed at and killed four girl coeds who were walking to their dorms from class, girls not even involved in the demonstration. Rubber bullets were supposed to be loaded, not shells used in war for killing.

Which party is the Bully Party? Did you see the Nazi style treatment at the 99% gatherings where bully policemen used pepper spray to saturated the heads and eyes of peaceful demonstrators sitting on the ground? Such cowards should be jailed or worse! One Gestapo reached around a girl to spray her behind her glasses. Do you want this type of demented person controlling America on every corner? They did the same type stuff under Hitler and Mussolini. The possibilities are very real. I'm not sure any of those doing those assaults was even arrested or tried. They may have been promoted! You can see how eager those public servants were to take out their personal anger on peaceful women demonstrators. What cowards!

Super Computers in Stock Trades Money in the stock market moves around. When someone loses someone else gains. The money doesn't go poof into the air. When stocks are sold profits (or losses) are locked in. Very rich persons have had super computers built which can buy and sell millions of shares every second. Some stocks are owned for only seconds then sold with profits of two hundredths of one cent. The purchase and sale of one million share yields $2000. The computers work around the clock. I think of this process as vacuuming wealth from the stock market in smaller amounts continuously.

It is not illegal and you cannot beat such competition. You may buy stocks and sell them making a profit, but you have to be very deliberate. You can lose, too. Most investors do.

Stocks can be purchased with imaginary money and investors can also place bets on stocks going down in price. The market can be shocked to scare stockholders into dumping their stocks at losses, which can then become another's gain. Insider information, although illegal, often assures an investor does well.

In essence everything is rigged. Gone are the days you could buy quality stocks and watch them grow over years.

Taxes Speaker of the House John Boehner said wanting to tax the rich "is class warfare. Wealthy people won't invest if taxes are added."
What a bunch of malarky. When the top rate was 91%, people invested regularly, maybe even more than now. Various polls indicate 82 to 90% of Americans think the rich should pay higher taxes. They use the government infrastructure and services much more than the poor, and.......why should someone making over a million or a billion pay less than a teacher, a

policeman, a plumber or a fireman? The formula should always include "a sense of fair play."

A Partial List of How to Move Wealth to the Rich
Cause a depression
Cause a recession
Foreclosures
Stock market manipulation
Cause thrift banks to fail
Cause banks to fail
Cause Wall St. firms and insurance companies to fail
A law (protected by GOP) saying hedge fund operators don't pay taxes
Favorable tax rates
Tax credits
Medicare fraud by scammers, not patients
Theft of war funds
Almost free shipping by businesses at U. S. P. S. (bulk business mail)
All forms of corporate welfare
Pension funds which employers allow to disappear
Superfund - to clean up toxic sites caused by businesses
Massive amounts FEMA funds to businesses and home owners; loses from hurricane flooding up Chesapeake Bay...GWB guaranteed rich businesses and homeowners 100% payment for all losses **prior** to the actual happening
$5/gallon military protection of oil companies worldwide
Fake non-profits
Free use by rich of canals, oil wells and such
Allowances on expensing of luxury items
Government loaning money to banks at very low rates (not bailouts)
Bailouts

Government paid research on drugs, and on many items including the fracking process which Halliburton tries to take credit for which was done at taxpayer expense, not by Halliburton
Free or almost free repatriation of foreign corporate profits (under G. W. B. for around 1%)

Gridlock in Congress Former President Bill Clinton was interviewed by Wolf Blitzer on CNN on September 24, 2011. Asked about the ever present gridlock, the daily fights in Congress, Bill replied, "Why are people surprised? The Tea Party and the Republicans campaigned exactly on that theme. Voters are getting exactly what they voted for, yet act surprised."

The New York State GOP Corporate Welfare Giveaway According to the front page story in "The Daily Star" on May 25, 2012 New York Senate Republicans put forth their New Jobs-NY Plan. Would anyone be surprised about the massive support by New York State? It seems to be patterned exactly like the Reagan, Bush and Bush plans which put us into The Great

Recession. The word "lunacy" pops into my mind. Imagine the cost to NYS from this list of corporate welfare.

* elimination of taxes on NYS manufacturers for three years
* a 20% cut in corporate tax rates for small businesses
* tax credits of up to $5000 for each "created job;" $8000 if the new employee was unemployed, and $10,000 for hiring a returning Veteran
* additional credits for small beer brewers

No projected costs were given for these and other items included in this bill. Most larger businesses readjusted several years ago and at this point are making solid profits, but if such offers are made, businesses certainly are not going to pass them up.

Future Population As centuries pass the population dilemma will become more intense. Debates will rage even more than they do now surrounding abortion and birth control rights. Rights' issues may change to needs' issues.

Down through history population control had been allowed, needed or whatever term fits with Hawaii being one example. The islands could support only X number of humans. Girl babies were taken to the ocean and drowned; at least that's what I remember from the movie, "Hawaii," many years ago.

Right up front I'll say I don't have many answers or suggestions other than conserving our limited resources, and through asking world citizens to voluntarily have fewer children. Of course birth control has to be a part of the plan. It would make sense even if resources were unlimited.

Right wing Republican Presidential candidate, former U. S. Senator Rick Santorum has been going wild with his Catholic stance against any form of birth control. Women and their thoughts are left out of the equation by Republicans, the male leaders in the Catholic Church, and basically all GOP males in Congress.

They take a stance any possible life is life to be protected. Dandruff is cells dropping off one's body and could be the source of a cloned person. I find it a bit hard to understand a church which is so strict on some values will allow young boys to be molested and used by priests. Not only does the Church suppress the knowing of it, it moves the pedophiles to new locations knowing they will continue molesting more boys. What values do those decisions show?

Humans are sexual beings by design. If Catholics are expected to increase the populations on Earth and "wasting seeds" is wrong, why does the Catholic Church forbid Priests and Nuns from marrying? To me it seems the "leaders" are ignoring their God's design.

I think religion can be a good thing, just not those who use religion to bully. For years I have said, "Jesus was the original liberal." Recently minutes after Congressional Republicans voted in unison to give oil companies $40 billion (40,000 million,) they then voted against $10 million for the WIC (Women, Infants, Children) to assist women needing a little help to possibly avoid an abortion. How can life be so important and not so important at the same time? An extra $40 billion in profits trumps any help for women, infants and children. I think Republicans like to hear themselves say they support life even though they don't show it when push comes to shove.

The GOP has accused colleges for a decrease in number of persons who believe in a religion here in the U. S. A. One does not have to be a brain surgeon to see the phoniness bantered about. Students choose not to associate with those who claim to be religious as they lie, connive and otherwise use religion to rev up their base. We can remember right wing dictator Adolf Hitler saying, "God is on our side!" Yup! He certainly was a Christian! The right wing in the U. S. is patterned after the fascist setup of Hitler and Mussolini. The similarities are identical right down to saying they are Christians!

Eventually a person's life will have to be weighed against the rights of the masses of world citizens. Like illegal immigration, it'll be tough and will continue to be kicked down the road a long time as "WaterWorld" happens.

Trust Me "There is no possible way these four nuclear generating plants could ever have a problem. Every possibility is covered thoroughly." That is what was said about the nuclear electric power generating plant in Japan. Don't forget Chernobyl and Three Mile Island.

British Petroleum assured President George W. Bush it had all the technology, all the equipment, all the help and all the materials available in the very unlikely event anything went wrong at the drill site in the Gulf of Mexico. Nobody verified the direct lies. In their recent television ads they mislead saying BP has appropriated $20 billion. They may have appropriated it but they have released only a small portion of it.

With natural gas drilling they show they use steel and concrete to secure wells from leaking. New York state was originally mostly under the ocean. The land has large supplies of salt in it. Salt is mined in the Syracuse area. Road crews can tell you both steel and concrete are dissolved by salt.

Twenty-two years ago an extremely intoxicated Captain of Exxon's Valdez hit a land mass causing a large oil spill. A judge assessed a $125 billion cleanup fee against Exxon. George W. Bush unilaterally cut it to $25 billion. To date Exxon continues getting billions in subsidies from us - and has never paid a penny toward the court order. How do you spell arrogance and stupidity?

"Our Republican Party took a $5.77 trillion surplus to a debt of $13 trillion. Each year another trillion in interest is added. We wrecked the economy, shipped over 50,000 U. S. factories out of the country, and lost millions of jobs. We have not proposed or allowed any job stimulus bills under President Obama while we have had control. We want to continue the same economic policies Republicans have advocated since Reagan was

President, and boy are we itching to get into some more wars like over in Syria! Trust us and elect Willard for President. Don't even believe former President Bill Clinton when he says Romney will create a big disaster if elected. What does he know about economics?" Does that sound like what a Republican should be saying?

What we do and represent leaches into the fabric of our family and greater community. It is the real part of us that lives on after our physical death. George Eastman created technology, the many factories to produce them, RIT, a hospital system, a great pension system, medical insurance and care, the first rolls of film, the first digital cameras, film for motion pictures and a strong middle class around Rochester, N. Y. George Eastman surely lives on.

Endicott Johnson Shoes and Corning, Inc. had similar pasts. What we do as we live, good or bad, becomes knitted into all related histories.

Squirrels Squirrels go through a ritual planting trees which will not bear nuts in their lifetimes. They eat from what their ancestors planted.

Donate Blood and Body Organs You can have your driver's license marked as an organ donor. You can also be a blood donor, for the need for blood donations is ever present. As a required project for a health class in college I went through a battle with the Red Cross in Syracuse after deciding to have a blood drive at The State University College at Oneonta, N. Y. For three weeks, The Red Cross told me they don't go to colleges. I had already gained permission from the College to have the blood drive in our new upper campus gymnasium.
The red Cross official finally agreed to give it a try. I signed up 175 students myself. Area people were invited through the newspaper. Students had to have written permission from a parent.
At 6:00 P. M. the Red Cross official announced to over 100 people in a wide, long line she was sorry but they had run out of glass collection bottles. They had brought only 250 bottles. I was told right there it was their most successful day ever for the American Red Cross.
Today they collect their most blood from college and high school campuses. A couple years ago they sent me a letter of recognition for 50 years of great success. That was a big moment for me. I have donated over 14 gallons since they started keeping track, so some of you reading this may have some of my blood in your arteries. Most of you can donate, too. You get over being scared after a time or two. This isn't really about politics but in a way it is. We are all dependent upon each other at times.

Bad Events When we see big events like hurricanes, tornados, floods or such we realize immediate help is needed. We as a country, can watch then ignore those persons without breaking any laws. But America is America and more is expected of a country with so much. Hours ago Turkey had a 7.6 earthquake. Should we ignore them and just wish them well? Being a conservative Democrat I look at such with compassion, and with reality.

The following assumes employees are paid a real, fair living wage. Some feel GM employees were overpaid with wages and benefits costing $85,000 to $106,000. GM made ungodly profits even with those employee costs which again were only a fraction of the profits they produced. The average U. S. employee's wages have dropped since 2001 by over $3000.

You have been conditioned to set your sights low. The profits are there for the corporations. According to two people who are in the position to know, Fortune 500 companies have net profits of $300,000 or more each year after all costs are deducted.

According to the news $27 trillion moved to the top 2% during President George W. Bush's eight years associated with the White House. Those monies included funds from the stock market, retirement funds and foreclosures.

Bernie Madoff was reported conducting a Ponzi scheme to the SEC twice. The Securities and Exchange fired the employee for pushing the case after The White House applied pressure.

Higher costs A variety of costs to you are higher because:
*illegal collusion cuts down on competition. (it appears gasoline companies don't operate in some states but others do)
*auto dealerships are buying out all competitors. (What auto dealership in Utica isn't owned by Don Carbone?)
*there is little real competition in the drug market, energy market and insurance market.
*Vice President Cheney held an energy policy meeting in private at government expense at a government facility, then refused to release notes, who was there or any other details of the meeting.
*hospitals, medical groups, funeral homes, cemeteries and creameries are being bought up by huge companies which don't compete much.
*cable t. v., phone service and internet providers are basically monopolies.
*stocks are bought and sold millions at a time by automatic computers for just seconds making your purchases and holdings fairly immaterial.

Republican Parallels With Muslims Republicans (not every one) overall have a diminished view of women, some even quote that authority from "The Bible." Women are to be subservient and servants to men.

Women in the Middle East must walk behind men, and only if given permission can they leave the home. They cannot drive and must wear burkas totally blocking their identity. A divorce happens if the husband says "I divorce you" three times. Until just about 100 years ago women could not even vote in America.

Muslim women cannot attend schools. Republican President Nixon wondered aloud why the U. S. wastes money educating women. Oddly, like certain Americans, Muslim women acquiesce to male domination saying if the "Koran" says it, it is o. k. with them.

Some women, some gays and lesbians, some Latinos, some Blacks, and many direly poor applaud and support the very party which very purposefully holds them down financially and power wise by keeping minimum wages below slave level, minimizing and retracting any employee benefits, and by busting labor unions which attempt to protect workers' rights. They are challenged by business unions such as the AGC (Association of General Contractors,) school board state and national unions, and Chambers of Commerce units among other business unions. The word union comes from uniting for a common purpose.

I will not hang a label on those of you who support the very ones downing and attempting to minimize you. Instead I will quote the polite statement made by Buffalo Bills' quarterback, Republican Senator Jack Kemp. He said, "Americans have the Constitutional right to be..wrong." You may replace the last word if you wish!

As long as we have willing participants carrying the water for and donating to millionaires and billionaires, the top 2% will become not only richer, but more powerful. Such a concentration of power in so few persons in the past has led to power grabs with bad endings too many times. There are reasons all civilizations eventually fall.

The following is a quote from Ben Franklin at the close of the Constitutional Convention in 1787, when asked what kind of government we would now have. He responded, "A Republic, if you can keep it." He was knowledgeable enough to know our democracy would be challenged from time to time. Will we care enough to believe in it and keep it for ourselves and our great-grandchildren?

More Ben Franklin quotes - to take a quick break from heavy thinking...

"Beer is proof that God loves us and wants us to be happy."

"In wine there is wisdom, in beer there is Freedom, in water there is bacteria."

"Man will occasionally stumble over the truth, but usually manages to pick himself up, walk over or around it, and carry on."

"The Constitution only guarantees the American people the right to pursue happiness. You have to catch it yourself."

"We are all born ignorant, but one must work hard to remain stupid."

You may want to Google Ben Franklin and go for the quotes. I am sure it will give you some laughs.

Immigration Solutions

Everyone knows the U. S. government's immigration policy has been one of turning a blind eye. I compare it to letting a couple poor fourth grade boys with baseball mitts in hand into a ball game without tickets. The ticket taker can easily guess the boys don't have the few bucks needed as they stand there looking in. What is the hurt? Being fans they will be buying hundreds of tickets after they have jobs.

Multi-millionaire farmers want employees who will work fast for little pay under harsh and unsafe, hot conditions. It is easy, also, to cheat them out of pay even at rates below minimum wage.

Homes and shopping centers will be built and repaired at low costs, lawns will be groomed for less, nannies hired for less, and fruits and vegetables are available at lower prices. Willard saves that way.

For over two years around 2006, Democrats tried to get the ball rolling on the unresolved immigration issues. An estimated 11,000,000 or more illegal Mexican immigrants are already here. Immigration laws were enforced about as much as Blue Laws saying you can't sell on a Sunday. Republicans did everything possible to block Democrats from hiring between 5000 and 7000 new border agents.

Having control of Congress for two years gave Democrats the opportunity to put the bill forth to President George W. Bush. A veto was expected so imagine the surprise when he signed it into law. Finally we could start getting a handle on the immigration issue.

Re-enlistments were down as were enlistments for troops to go to Bush's elective wars in Iraq and Afghanistan. In an unprecedented act, President Bush sent the troops to Iraq. Immigration continued to be ignored.

Republicans like to talk and look tough. That explains talking strongly about immigration while keeping the status quo so farmers and home builders can keep laborers they can abuse. Even Willard Romney had illegal immigrants tending to his property's lawn and shrubs. He claimed he didn't know they were illegal. Sure! If so why did he make such as issue of trying to keep it quiet?

Affordable Care Act

Healthcare is another kick the can down the road issue. President Obama campaigned on getting that done. He was elected to get it done which is what he did. When money equal to one-eighth of our $15.0128 trillion gross national product (GNP) is involved we are talking around TWO TRILLION DOLLARS. Another way of putting that is 2,000 billion; or 2,000,000 million dollars are spent on American healthcare each year. A big two-thirds of that is skimmed off as profits by healthcare insurance companies which are owned by wealthy investors who are almost 100& Republicans.

Does that give you a little idea why they have such an extreme interest in getting you upset and against the Affordable Care Law? It is all about the M-O-N-E-Y! They have claimed it has made insurance costs go up. The money part hasn't even kicked in yet - and - if you are on Medicare a recovered $500,000,000,000 going to insurance companies for absolutely no reason (was put in by Republicans) has been redirected into lowering the size of the donut hole which would cut the amount you will have to pay if your costs reach the donut hole level. They are great alarmists and may I say HUGE liars!

Most people really like Social Security and Medicare. If you do, you will really like The Affordable Care Act. Don't believe the lie when Republicans say Democrats stole the $500 billion. That is whacked thinking! Except for just before elections Republicans want to destroy Social Security and Medicare. As they are doing with the Affordable Care Act, they opposed Social Security and Medicare at the times those were started by Democrats. As Grover Norquist, who represents Republicans said, "Let's cripple them enough so I can drown them in a both tub!"

DON'T BE BULLIED!

DON'T ACCEPT LIES!

LEARN THE TRUTH!

Canadian Prime Minister - 2012

The leaders of Mexico and Canada met in Washington as guests of President Obama earlier this year. Given a reporter's question about getting along with the U. S. leadership, Canada's Prime Minister carefully spoke of having great cooperation for the past three years. In stark contrast he made no mention of working with President George W. Bush. The silent pause was telling.

Some things to think about~~~Ideas to consider

If possible join a credit union instead of using banks. Some may not handle mortgages but most do. YOU are an owner of the credit union. Profit is not the motive. There are so many advantages, and rates on loans are way lower than you would think possible.

Long range employees should not miss opportunities to buy and own, as a group, the company they work for. Profits you help make come back to you. I am not necessarily talking about buying company stock as in a 401-K. Employees don't get much say in such cases.

A person with a job with a real living wage doesn't lose hope and go rob a bank as a last resort. Killings can result as plans go wrong magnifying the problems. A job gives a person purpose and pride besides money for basics, and hopefully some extras.

Stop shipping our jobs to other countries. This should apply to Presidents especially. Every company which manufactures here in the U. S. should be required to pay taxes here. Repeal laws which allowed Romney and Quayle to profit from exporting our financial base. Some of us try to protect America; some work at destroying it! They have no respect from me!

Make yacht owners and anyone with a boat or ship who uses the Erie Canal free pay the true real costs of their canal use instead of pushing the costs onto the NYS Thruway users. Guess who writes such things into law to save the rich from paying?

Do not allow any company which has purposefully scammed our government, to gain another contract. Period. Always get the money back from such payments already made. Let's get rid of the attitude of, "The money is gone. Let's not do that again." That invites every company to be crooked. What is the downside?

The SEC needs a more effective way to stop insider trading. It appeared to be rampant from 2001 through 2009. Some people are hired to hang around Congress just to overhear private conversations. Super listening devices are easy to buy and use. Computer programs could find those who are using insider information.

When a President lies to get us into a war he or she should be tried for treason - for it is treasonous behavior causing deaths and injuries of our troops. Any officials being a part of the scheme should be tried right along with the President. There is no fear from being prosecuted for anything. Justice is to be fair and equal. Criminals should be treated as criminals. I am fortunate both of my grandsons stationed in Afghanistan returned safely. Some of their fellow troops didn't do as well. They aren't just fellow troops; they were real persons with names, families, hopes and dreams, there because of ego trips and greed.

Is the Republican Judge Kenneth Starr, who is now a "guest" in a federal prison for multiple felonies the same person who viscously prosecuted President Clinton for lying about a personal matter? I hope so. If so, he was ironically appointed to the bench by President Clinton in a non-political appointment, which theoretically, is the way it is supposed to be.

Reward persons who turn in solid information exposing scamming of customers. Those customers should include government purchases. Back-charge the costs to the scammer. Communications and computer equipment manufacturers would possibly straighten up. Also, include computer security companies. I have stood my ground on three such issues. I have received repeated phone calls, calls with extremely loud screeching sounds, and calls which have been intended to intimidate me. They never use a phone with a listed number. I do have recordings of some of them. Enough is enough!

Make it a law hedge fund profits must be taxed. 22 hedge fund persons made a total of $27 billion in a year. Republican laws protect them from having to pay taxes. Democrats have had a continued fight with Republicans over this item. If you gave The House and Senate more Democratic members, it could happen. We could get our country back on course similar to the way President Clinton did. It isn't that hard. All we need to do is use common sense and fair play.

In a time when I guess inflation was over 10%, my mother had to pay taxes on the small interest she received on a savings account at maybe 3%. She had actually lost buying power. No interest should be taxable until it reaches the real cost of living increase figure. Since interest paid is seldom more than the cost of living, it shouldn't be taxed at all. It would possibly encourage some to save more toward an emergency. Banks would be saved from sending out 1099's to show Sally Jones received $3.12 in interest; and I. R. S. computers would need less memory. I haven't thought this through completely, but it may have some merit.

Charge businesses the same as it charges everybody else for services of the United States Post Office. It is ridiculous for someone to be able to send thousands of over-length tubes, which will not fit into most mailboxes, for 5 cents each. If a business can't make it by paying standard rates maybe they should close down. What do they do with all those "shipping and handling charges?" The Post Office doesn't get much of it.

I might make the exception when it comes to second class mail, newspapers and magazines. I consider them in an educational category, and education is good for America and the world. A reduced rate would be fine with me for these items. That, too, needs more thought.

The NYS Taylor Law is one of the most unfair laws ever written. Teachers do not want to strike but bottom line they should be afforded the same rights everyone else has. If a teacher does not show up for work during a strike he or she naturally is not paid for that day. The Taylor Law stipulates the teacher will lose three more days pay for every day on strike, so the teacher loses 4 days pay.

There is absolutely no penalty of any sort applied to the school or the school board. Because of that they don't come to an agreement for years. I have seen many contracts stalled on purpose for 4 or 5 years. Then when retro pay is given there is no interest. What part of that system is fair as they choose to "punish teachers?"

I suggest school boards be immediately forced to pay teachers an additional non-refundable 10% after the first full week without a contract following an official suggestion made by a recognized third party. The nonsense would stop in short order. Presumably a lot of time has already passed by the time it gets to arbitration. A board ought to be able to make a decision within a week after an arbitrator renders a decision.

Taxes should be apportioned according to who uses and benefits from the government paid program or service.

Employees should be paid at least enough to meet all normal basic needs.

We need to do as much as possible to stop the destruction of rain forests. We, and other wealthy countries should even pay to have the destruction of thousands of acres each day stopped. From rough figures seven pounds of home heating fuel burning (oxidizing) yields 19 pounds of carbon dioxide (CO_2) which can be absorbed by plants during photosynthesis. Most of carbon dioxide is oxygen. We can't survive without the oxygen being released. It is that simple. Typical air contains 20% oxygen. Mountain climbers and pilots experience breathing difficulties when the oxygen supply is less. Without enough plants on Earth human and animal breathing will get closer to breathing as if you have COPD. Autos and heating systems will not work correctly. Oxygen will become a big commodity.

After we all die plants will grow and replenish the oxygen. Remember all the dinosaurs died when the dust from an asteroid which hit the Earth blocked the sunlight so all vegetation died. No plants to eat and not enough oxygen. Have you noticed how many people are now having breathing problems? Have you ever wondered why? We also now have acid air besides acid rain.

As humans we have the mental abilities to see and figure things out. We can do something about a problem or just live with it and see. Ignoring something makes us ignorant.

Almost every glacier has melted and the oceans are higher, so high some low islands have had to be abandoned, but most Republicans deny global warming. I use these as examples of the type of attitude and thinking which keeps problems from being addressed. Eventually the problems will be extreme. I'm trying to educate you, not scare you.

There is time to change things but it won't happen unless enough of you show you care, and you elect legislators who aren't in their own la-la land ignoring reality. Those owning rainforest lands want to profit from selling the logs and from growing crops and cattle on the land. In reality they are large corporations, all names you would recognize. You can easily Google "Rainforest."

An average of 200,000 acres are burned every day in the Amazon Rainforest, a rate which will eliminate the rainforest there in 40 years. Trees grown there contain some of the best cancer medicine in the world. As in the movie, "Avatar," the beneficial trees will be gone through stupidity and greed.

To give you an idea in simple form, how much photosynthesis takes place in one tree, consider a large maple tree transpires (gives off) 250 gallons of water a day. The carbon is taken from the CO_2 releasing the oxygen into the air as part of a cycle. In the presence of chlorophyll and with some minerals the carbon is transformed into a sugary sap, plant food.

Long term jail is no answer for illegal drug use in most cases. I am sure doctors and other professionals with input from users and some who have successfully come through rehab can come up with success without all the costs of trials and incarceration. If only some could get their heads out of the punishment mode. Society wastes so much time and money getting into peoples' lives. Isn't that what Republicans complain about, others butting into their lives? Then they want to tell people they can't use any birth control, or marijuana, or can't do this or that. They are one screwed up tribe, aren't they! I make these comments as one who has never used marijuana or illegal drugs. Honest.

I think marijuana should be regulated like cigarettes. Telling people to stop using marijuana is like telling everyone to stop eating pizza. I don't think either will happen. Meanwhile people see themselves as criminals who eventually don't care. It weakens our system of laws.

Eighteen year old drivers could be issued either a night driver's license, or a "drinking license." It really isn't a license to drink but one with a drinking right at age 18, and in the process forfeiting the right to drive after 10:00 P. M. The night driving license portion would be revoked to being restricted to only daytime driving until age 21 if the license holder were convicted of any DWI or DWAI. The same would apply with the "drinking license." A judge could allow an exception for certain job or school related issues providing a second offense doesn't occur.

There are many ways education and the running of schools could be rethought for saving money, and for expanding the educational benefit. I think there could be a final study hall period of the day in which homework could be done by most students without having to take any or much home. The library and computers could be used extensively. If students could leave school and have a life as a child without homework it would benefit them mentally and socially.

Another option would be to encourage those who want to stay, to remain in school in a quiet room where completing homework is easier than at home. Some schools already run a late bus, or possibly the student could just walk home. We should not miss a chance to use the school as much as possible.

Going to school for a half day several days a year is ridiculous in terms of costs and efficiency. It is done to establish a minimum number of days in school to figure state aid to the district. A plan should be able to be presented to the State Education Department which would hopefully have an open mind in resetting needed changes for better education and to save money and energy.

Most every school should be equipped with heat pumps for heat and hot water, and for cooling (AC) on warmer days. It would cut energy costs drastically and set a good example for the community. Solar panels installed over a black tar roof could allow electricity to be generated some of which could be sold. During the summer months the income should be even more impressive. Careful installation could assure snow is shed from the units more efficiently. Or the space could be leased to a private company to produce income for the school. Overall, a good example would be set. Perhaps BOCES' students could learn the trade by installing the units: heat pumps and solar panels.

School could be run year round as 4 semesters (or quarters.) Students and teachers would attend three of the four quarters. Obviously, students and teachers would have different starting dates. It would be set up more like college and subjects could be broken into 3 levels instead of just one. If a student failed one quarter he or she would repeat the 3 months, not a whole year. With the building being used 25% more, a smaller physical school would suffice rather than having to enlarge the school. I know a senior trip or a prom would be a little more difficult but not impossible.

If a teacher or a family wanted to go on a trip or live in another area during the winter, for instance, some flexibility could be afforded. Places like Disney World would not be so flooded at particular times as much as it is now.

Some families may want to go on an extended skiing vacation; or to Europe.. With cheap AC school in summer may be a good thing; no coats, boots, hats, gloves, etc. And physical ed. classes could have more outdoor softball rather than indoor dodgeball.

For some students there could be actual on the job training (OJT) allowing students to get hands-on training while drawing some pay, too. Very possibly some students may end up working for that company during vacations or after graduation. I see too many students go to expensive BOCES' classes without acquiring any skills. I've watched most stand around while one or two and the teacher worked. That teaches too many bad things about life.

Having taught the learning disabled I know many cannot read very well. It isn't from a teacher not doing a good job. Boys in particular are learning disabled in reading decoding or in reading comprehension...or both. The Library of Congress has recorded books and textbooks available for any person with a reading disability. I can tell you my L. D. students smiled a lot after I set them up with the Library of Congress in Albany, N. Y. for tapes of any book, including textbooks.

Today it is probably even easier because of being able to send books through the internet instantly.

I do not know about Microsoft, but I do know an Apple computer can read any printed writing aloud in any language. If written in French, for example, you can have it read to you in English or Chinese with any accent you want. Any language can be read in any language you chose.

We need to have our students take advantage of this spectacular technology. I suggest a teacher let a computer read a portion of a social studies or science text during class time now and then. I am L. D. in reading decoding. I would have loved it if that had been done for me. Reading is a project for me sometimes. Being able to read fluently is a gift you may not even appreciate if it has always been that way for you.

This suggestion is a big one. The success could be overwhelming in this day and age when college costs are going out of sight. Many school populations are diminishing. Area school buildings now have extra rooms and extra teachers which could serve other purposes.

Two of the larger costs in going to college are meals and room. Today's high school students are being taught way beyond what students were taught even 20 years ago. Some high school students leave high school with college credits already, which is great.

I believe high schools could be financially encouraged to teach the basic college courses taking the student to his or her junior college level. The student lives at home, eats meals at home, drives a family vehicle or rides to "college" on the school bus. Parents will have more input into the child's drug and alcohol use. The student may have a better chance to obtain a job in his or her own community if an income is necessary. Everything seems like a positive. Another big deal is the school gets a needed infusion of lots of money. Colleges could pay to have space available in a high school, and tuition could be at a reduced rate.

Teachers now have to have a Masters Degree which takes at least another year beyond the fourth year. Lawyers, doctors, pharmacists and dentists all have to go to college for at least seven years. I believe this college at high school could be easily made to work.

Schools and public buildings are built to specs written a long time ago. Coal was cheap so rooms were built with high ceilings providing many cubic yards of air for each student per hour. On top of that every room has an air exchanger which pretty much pumps air from outdoors into the classroom constantly. That air might be 35 degrees below zero.

A taller building costs much more to build, much more to heat or cool, and much more to maintain. You will notice the same thing in your Walmart or your grocery store. Those outdated regulations cover all public buildings. All the regulations need to be updated. Energy is getting more expensive and at some point reality has to be recognized and energy saved for the future.

An Important Item

A big change we could have economically in America would be to change how we look at monies doled out by our governments. I will state this as simply as I can for the concept is very simple.

The words corporate welfare are pervasive within these pages. The billions and trillions are staggering and in so many cases unnecessary. Other payments are emergency help to those who have lost a job and in simple terms need a boost to get past a time of trouble.

Businesses and workers, as a matter of course, hit hard times. Whether General Motors or Jim Smith, interim help can be lifesaving. With some, it is not the same. There is not much chance for recovering monies from some currently on welfare but I believe it could work in most cases.

I very much backed President Clinton's "two years max" welfare. It didn't lack compassion but it surely was effective. Some people do misuse the system. I recognize that and don't support it.

The same is true for corporate welfare. They have no shame in continuing with their hands out for more despite how high profits are.

How much would it take to buy you if someone asked you to to change beliefs which are ingrained in your head? CEO's must have a tolerance which allows them to take the money regardless of what might embarrass 99% of the people. This book is a book of shame for them.

Corporate welfare and welfare to people should be considered a repayable loan in most every case. The acceptance of it would automatically register the transaction as a loan, not a gift.

For people a percentage of their income would be recovered for the federal treasury automatically. Compassion would be shown as the debt is collected over a long period of time, unless, of course, the person wins the Lottery. In such a case payment in full would happen then.

Before a person or a business could receive a loan, a signature or signatures would be required to allow the government to seize assets, if necessary, to assure repayment. Boards of directors would also have to pledge their own assets. If they protest their application should be dropped. They aren't being forced to take the loan, but taxpayers are being forced to put their monies forward to be loaned. No dividends should be paid until the debt is repaid.

If honestly in trouble from which they can recover, they should be tickled to receive the loan. The same is true for families which need money for foods and necessities. I imagine I would be extremely pleased to get the needed help; and would not have a problem in repaying it.

It may take a few years before both sides have a change in the mentality of not having to repay it. I think that would be especially true with the corporations. They have been getting big chunks of free pork for decades and will fight this change with everything they've got. That would only indicate how successful it has been for them for many decades. "Welfare" recipients would not have to be spied on, so counties would need fewer agents.

Exxon-Mobil would be required to pay its bill with interest and no parts of $40 billion would flow in its direction. Hopefully, stupidity and Republican greed laws would be eliminated. As a taxpayer I am tired of being abused every day. Maybe The Tea Party will join me in this huge change. They want less money spent as I do. I invite Tea Partiers to side with me about not allowing rich people to avoid taxes through any form of a Bush tax cut.

As an example a farm equipment dealer making millions in profits from poor farmers has had 12 years of tax breaks. Now Republicans want that law to become permanent. Tell me why a dealer making 25 to 35% profits on his sales, according to my economics' classes, and even more on parts and labor should be given continuous hugh tax breaks. How can someone justify making $20,000 or more in selling you a tractor? You may work an entire year to make that much.

If a government official came to your town and took money from your pockets, then walked over and handed it to the equipment dealer, would you remain passive and o. k. about it? Or would you be steamed? That is exactly what the Bush tax cuts do. And that is after he made a huge profit from you. You need to deal in reality.

Dealers need no incentives to stay in business - and at your expense. As a child I worked on farms until I was 18, so I know how hard you work. I appreciate you. You need to help me help you and in the process save America.

Profitable businesses given (Loaned) funds would have monies collected from them automatically the same way it would be taken from people.

Is this a possible way to get us out of the tax funk which has not been getting any better?

We could pay off our national debt in short order. Businesses should be able to operate without subsidies. A good idea should eventually be profitable and should attract private investment. I know some businesses we need are more on the risky side (like the manufacture of solar panels,) especially in a world market. Loans, with tight controls, could be in order but only after hard consideration. No more stiffing American taxpayers. How can anyone be opposed to that? I already know who would be.

Chapter 12 IS DEMOCRACY WORTH SAVING?

As we witnessed last year during the Arab Spring in northern Africa, there was a thirst for freedom and rights taken from them for decades by dictators who ruled over them with an iron grip. Emotions ran high as citizens from countries like Egypt and Libya saw chances of becoming democracies.

Some interviewed recalled their lives as "living dead" as their lives were completely controlled. Offending a dictator could bring a bulldozer to evacuate a long trench opened to contain the bodies of a family and its friends and neighbors. That is how dictators maintain control - through fear.

Even now as new elections are taking place, remnants of the old power base are still having impact. Democracy is still a distant hope, a work in progress; yet it instills hope in the hopeless.

We are America, a country seen as the epitome of hope for all people on Earth. In 1933, there was the failed coup to make America a fascist dictatorship. Most Americans had been against fascism, and in fighting in World War II had made that clear. Despite that, there were and still are those who liked and still like a fascist government of, by and for the corporations. Republicans are a distinct minority party with 31.25% of registered voters, yet because of their methods, slick publicity and mixing truth and fiction, and mountains of money, they actually control America with a firm hand.

A boa constrictor kills not by squeezing but by not allowing its prey to breathe. Every time there is an exhale it moves in until there is no room for inhaling. Democracy is being killed the same way.

So many Americans are beaten - their homes, jobs and retirements gone. The Supreme Court is now loaded 5 to 4 with "judges" who are legislating from the bench, The House is firmly Republican and will be unless we reverse it in November's election, and The Senate can't pass anything because of the 60 vote rule there. Democrats have a number around 55 but can't get any Republicans to help reach the number 60.

In affect Republicans control everything except for the few things President Obama can do without Congress. Even in that case the Supreme Court is overly eager to rule against him.

If ever there were a time for another dictatorship coup to be attempted it is now. They suffered no harm when they tried it in 1933. What do they have to lose? You can bet any such matters brought about in treason cases will be overturned in the current Supreme Court. Those interested in a coup don't care about lives or what they have to do to meet success.

Republicans as a group have no appreciation for hard work. Workers are like horses to them, totally disposal when no longer useful. Have you heard of many dictators who don't have histories of mass killings? As in Texas, executions are a part of the weekly schedule.

It may be hard to get a busy Democrat to get out and vote. I have heard, "My vote won't count for anything." That is totally wrong. Those yearning for freedom risk their lives to go vote and have a finger stained. When on television they showed the stained finger as a source or pride and restored hope.

There is no profit motive in writing this book. My hope is I can get you to go out and vote every time including the Tuesday this November.

Republicans vote religiously. That is where they get their power. They are led to believe they are the smart ones. There is a lust for power to be able to control the dumb, unfortunate herd. They need to take off the blinders so they can view the swath of their destruction they have been leaving. As their numbers continue to shrink from 85% to 31% they have found they need to use drastic measures to maintain. And they will not be embarrassed!

Democrats have 30% more registered voters than Republicans have registered voters; and we constantly lose elections. We believe the best ideas flow from discussions which can get heated at times. Some see that as weakness. I don't. Discussions yield better choices. We want to represent all the people even the rich.

The GOP has no ideas, but vote in unison for ideas passed down which will help them win and please the rich who fund them heavily. If you can't see and be upset by the damage they have done to America again, there is no hope.

Humorist and author Will Rogers once stated, "I don't belong to any organized political party...I'm a Democrat." Our first step in organizing is to learn and talk it up, then without fail take your friends to the booths and vote for Democrats. We have no doubt what and who Republicans stand for, and what and who Democrats stand for. The gap is so wide.

Most Republicans have much higher incomes from my observations. By voting they can calculate somewhat how much a party win can save them, so they have that incentive. Before I enlisted in the United States Air Force, I went through the mental process of knowing I may be called upon to give my life to protect what America represents. Taking a few minutes to go vote for the country I love is a much easier mental process.

Thank you to every person who wore a U. S. military uniform and served the America we love. If given the chance I'd shake your hand and thank you in person, especially those of you and your families who have suffered so horribly.

Be kind to someone today.